AF379178

Counterpoint

Counterpoint
Sculpture, Music, and Walter De Maria's *Large Rod Series*

Edited by Gavin Delahunty

with essays by
Gavin Delahunty
Caitlin Haskell

with contributions by
Chelsea Pierce
Jason Treuting

and installation notes by
Walter De Maria

Dallas Museum of Art
Distributed by Yale University Press, New Haven and London

Contents

Director's Foreword

Counterpoint: Sculpture, Music, and Walter De Maria's Large Rod Series is one of only a handful of catalogues published to date that showcase the highly regarded but rarely seen work of Walter De Maria (American, 1935–2013). Associated with the Minimal, Conceptual, and Land Art movements, he is best known for his large-scale outdoor works such as *The Lightning Field* (1977). This book explores De Maria's multifaceted achievements by way of his *Large Rod Series*, a body of ten polished metal floor-based sculptures made between 1984 and 1989. Almost two years in the making, the research presented here brings together a number of unpublished materials and photographs to achieve a fuller appreciation and understanding of this elusive artist.

The catalogue was conceived by Gavin Delahunty, the DMA's Hoffman Family Senior Curator of Contemporary Art, to celebrate De Maria's work and also to commemorate the co-acquisition of his *Large Rod Series: Circle/Rectangle 5, 7, 9, 11, 13* (1986) and *Pure Polygon Series* (1975–1976) by the Dallas Museum of Art with the San Francisco Museum of Modern Art in the spring of 2016. We would like to extend our sincere thanks to our colleagues leading the acquisition at SFMOMA: Gary Garrels, Elise S. Haas Senior Curator of Painting and Sculpture, and Caitlin Haskell, Assistant Curator of Painting and Sculpture. Without their immediate and enthusiastic response to the project, the acquisition—and this publication—would not have been possible.

The catalogue also marks the first installation of the work at our respective institutions. In the fall of 2016, the DMA presented the *Large Rod Series: Circle/ Rectangle 5, 7, 9, 11, 13* alongside El Greco's *Saint Francis Kneeling in Meditation* (1605–1610), generously on loan from the Meadows Museum. Completing the installation was a looped version of De Maria's musical composition, *Cricket Music* (1964). Experienced together, the sculpture, painting, and sound recording formed a new and distinctive meditation on themes of Minimalism, mathematics, progression, and sensory perception, their installation in an encyclopedic museum drawing parallels between artistic forms and iconographies of past and present.

We relied heavily on the generosity of the public and private owners of the ten works that complete the series to illustrate this first in-depth publication, and we would like to express our gratitude to them for their assistance: the Moderna Museet and Magasin III, Stockholm; Kiasma, Helsinki; Frances Bowes; Heiner Friedrich; Larry Gagosian; Louise and Leonard Riggio; and Philip and Rosella Rolla.

At the Walter De Maria Archives, we extend our warmest thanks to Elizabeth Childress, Director, and Michael Childress, Assistant to the Director, both of whom have been unflagging in their support and extraordinarily generous with their comprehensive knowledge of the artist.

We sincerely thank Cindy and Howard Rachofsky and TWO x TWO for AIDS and Art, without whose sustained encouragement and support this installation and catalogue would not have been possible. Our gratitude also goes to Larry Gagosian and Kara Vander Weg of Gagosian Gallery, who have been crucial to and completely supportive of our endeavor. We are deeply grateful to TWO x TWO for AIDS and Art and to the Gagosian Gallery for underwriting the costs associated with producing this publication.

We are much indebted to our contributing essayists Gavin Delahunty and Caitlin Haskell for the far-reaching ideas expressed in their texts. While De Maria's sculptural practice forms the basis of this book, what started as a consideration of a single work of art has led to unique lines of inquiry that we hope expand upon how we approach the *Large Rod Series*. Our thanks go to pianist Seth Knopp and percussionist Jason Treuting, whose passion and expertise guided us and helped illuminate both De Maria's musical compositions and the rhythmic workings of his sculptural practice.

We thank Miko McGinty of Miko McGinty, Inc., for the book's elegantly minimalist design and feel; Ellen Hirzy for her perceptive editing; and Patricia Fidler and Roland Coffey at Yale University Press for their assistance in distributing this title.

At the Dallas Museum of Art, we thank Eric Zeidler, Publications Manager; Tamara Wootton Forsyth, Associate Director of Collections, Exhibitions, and Facilities Management; and Joni Wilson-Bigornia, Exhibitions Manager, for their important contributions to this undertaking. We further acknowledge Nolan Jimbo, Temporary Projects Coordinator; Carol Griffin, Associate Registrar for Acquisitions and Deaccessions; Mary Balthrop, General Counsel; Giselle Castro-Brightenburg, Imaging Department Manager; Jill Bernstein, Director of Communications and Public Affairs; Cynthia Calabrese, Director of Development; Brad Flowers, Head Photographer; Ira Schrank, Photographer; John Lendvay, Head Preparator; Lance Lander, Manager of Gallery Technology and Innovation; Anne Lenhart, former Registrar for Collections; Tyler Livingston, Manager of Digital Rights and Intellectual Property; Kevin Parmer, Exhibition Graphic Designer; and Kimberly Daniell, Senior Manager of Communications, Public Affairs, and Social Media Strategy. Chelsea Pierce, Curatorial Assistant for the Contemporary Art Department, deserves a special acknowledgment for her excellent work compiling an exhibition history for the *Large Rod Series* and for her assiduous and untiring assistance throughout the project.

We owe our greatest expression of appreciation to Walter De Maria for his uncompromising yet ultimately universal art. It is our hope that this catalogue and the accompanying installation will introduce a wider public to De Maria's achievements and legacy.

Agustín Arteaga
The Eugene McDermott Director

Walter De Maria: Soundtrack to a Sculptor
Gavin Delahunty

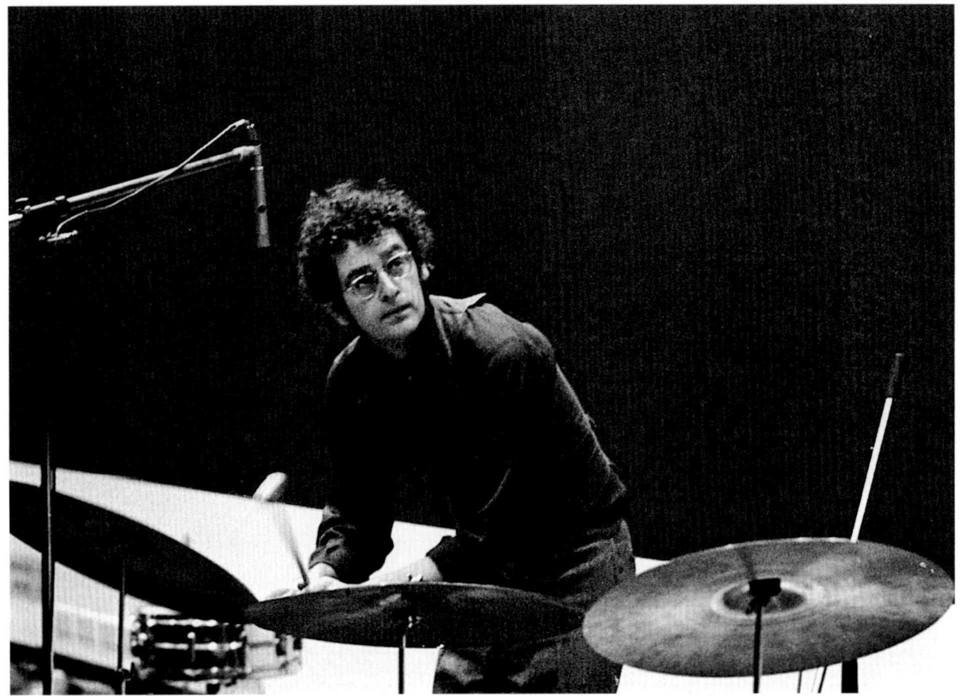

Fig. 1. Walter De Maria recording *Ocean Music* in London, 1968

"Well it all really started with the music, taking piano lessons at an early age and then later dropping that and studying drums, percussion, playing in the school orchestras and then playing in the school dance bands, getting into popular music and then even at age sixteen joining the Musicians Union."[1]

—Walter De Maria, 1972

When he was a high school student in the Bay Area during the early 1950s, Walter De Maria ran for office as a student representative. He was an unpopular candidate, described by fellow student Dennis Oppenheim as mysterious, nonconformist, sensitive, and almost dangerous.[2] After the other students took to the stage to give their speeches, De Maria prepared to deliver his own manifesto. But instead of addressing his audience as expected, he set up his drum kit and chanted his name repeatedly to a rhythmic beat. Oppenheim described De Maria's performance as "mesmerizing," like "early Steve Reich or Philip Glass . . . serial music." For his peers, De Maria's stunt must have been fascinating and infuriating in equal measure. Perhaps it was a cynical commentary on the futility of student elections or an astute observation that success in such a context is achieved by those who repeat a mantra and shout it the loudest. Whatever the purpose, this unrecorded and little-known performance highlights De Maria's longstanding interest in percussion and prefigures his forays into musical composition, which extended into the 1960s.

At the beginning of that decade, when Minimalism was taking its initial form in visual art, De Maria was working on his recording *Cricket Music* (1964). Twenty-four minutes long, the composition precedes De Maria's more familiar sculptural works and is a virtuoso exercise in rhythmic drumming to which has been added the sound of chirping crickets. This essay approaches the artist's work by revisiting the compositional structure and patterns of *Cricket Music* and the later composition *Ocean Music* (1968) in the belief that they illuminate his broader artistic practice (fig. 1). An examination of the importance of music to De Maria before its abrupt disappearance from his work sets the stage for a discussion of his better-known sculptures. De Maria's interest in percussion and avant-garde music—particularly the work of La Monte Young—was fundamental to his development into a key figure in the history of Minimalism.

Although the term came into use much later, Minimalism in music is widely understood to have begun with La Monte Young's *Trio for Strings* of 1958.[3] Fifty-eight minutes long, the *Trio* established Young as the first composer to adopt a truly Minimal language. It is cast in a single movement, with a haunting reliance on long, sustained tones. In his programming notes, Young describes how the instruments' sequences of pitches are not designed to be played "as individual *parts* but as contributions to a chordal unit whose components are of different durations." Young also stipulated "the production of a smooth, steady bow direction so that the long sustained tones sound as uninterrupted as possible." The effect has been likened to sculpture, "reinforced in performances by the statuesque appearance of the players."[4] As his primary influence, Young cited gagaku, a form of Japanese ceremonial music described in the *Harvard Dictionary of Music* as "characterized by smoothness, serenity, and precise execution without virtuosic display."

Young had arrived as a graduate student at the University of California, Berkeley, in September 1958 and had quickly established himself among his fellow students as a singular and innovative composer. At Berkeley he wrote several more scores and held multiple performances, both formal and informal. Among them was "Collaboration Event: to," a pair of concerts organized in partnership with the department of architecture.[5] The three performers were Young, Terry Riley, and percussionist Walter De Maria, who described Young as "the only person . . . of any consequence" that he met at Berkeley.[6]

De Maria's friendship with Young ultimately influenced his decision to move to New York in October 1960. There he immediately fell in with a group of like-minded musicians, composers, poets, choreographers, filmmakers, and artists who formed the downtown avant-garde. In July 1961 his exhibition *Boxes, Ropes, Explicit directions and demonstrations* was presented alongside solo shows by Young, Henry Flynt, Ray Johnson, Yoko Ono, and Yvonne Rainer at AG Gallery as part of a series of evenings devoted to individual artists. In 1963 he became the drummer in the short-lived pop band The Druds, with Young on saxophone, Patty Oldenburg as lead vocalist, Larry Poons on guitar, and Andy Warhol and Lucas Samaras as backup vocalists; Jasper Johns wrote the band's lyrics.[7] Later that year De Maria curated a program of exhibitions, film screenings, and performances with Robert Whitman at 9 Great Jones Street.[8] Throughout the early 1960s he performed as part of a musical ensemble with Young. This collaboration would later incorporate the likes of Marian Zazeela, Tony Conrad, and John Cale. In 1963 De Maria was included in "An Anthology," a special issue of *Beatitude East* magazine devoted to the avant-garde with which he was associated. Designed by George Maciunas, the issue featured twenty-five contributors, from established Fluxus artists to those newer on the scene. De Maria had exhibited in a benefit for the project the previous year, along with George Brecht, John Cage, Dick Higgins, Simone Forti, Charlotte Moorman, and Larry Poons. "An Anthology" has been described as "among the most influential collections of music and performance art of the 1960s, . . . representing an unprecedented breaking down of barriers between artistic media that had an important influence on the Fluxus movement."[9]

At the same time as these projects and collaborations, De Maria was constructing some of the earliest known examples of Minimalist sculpture, including *Ball Drop* (fig. 2). The ball or sphere in *Ball Drop* would develop as an important symbol for De Maria, like the square, circle, rectangle, cross, and swastika. Reflecting the influence of music on his work, *Ball Drop* incorporates an acoustic element. A brown, rectangular, coffin-like plywood box accommodates two square openings on its front face. Both are centrally positioned, one just above eye level and one approximately waist high. Instructions on the box invite the participant to take a wooden ball about the size of a grapefruit that rests in the lower opening and place it into the opening above (fig. 3). Without pause, the ball drops from the upper hole to the lower one, striking the plywood frame and producing a loud crack. You feel a peculiar, childlike compulsion to repeat the process—and humor when you do—that seems to derive from the combination of the work's plain symmetrical proportions and the arbitrary nature of the game. De Maria described his rectangular boxes as frames "isolating the reality inside, or non-reality."[10] Edward Strickland suggests that *Ball Drop* could be read as a Minimalist manifesto that undermines illusionism and metaphor with its blunt demonstration of weight and gravity: "It is not only the unknown nature of the interior of the box that provokes expectations of intriguing complexity but the status of the box in the gallery as a transcendental object. . . . When we drop the ball into the fetishized box in the middle of the gallery . . . we expect convoluted marvels instead of elementary physics."[11] Such expectations are confounded by the deadpan action of *Ball Drop*—the abrupt

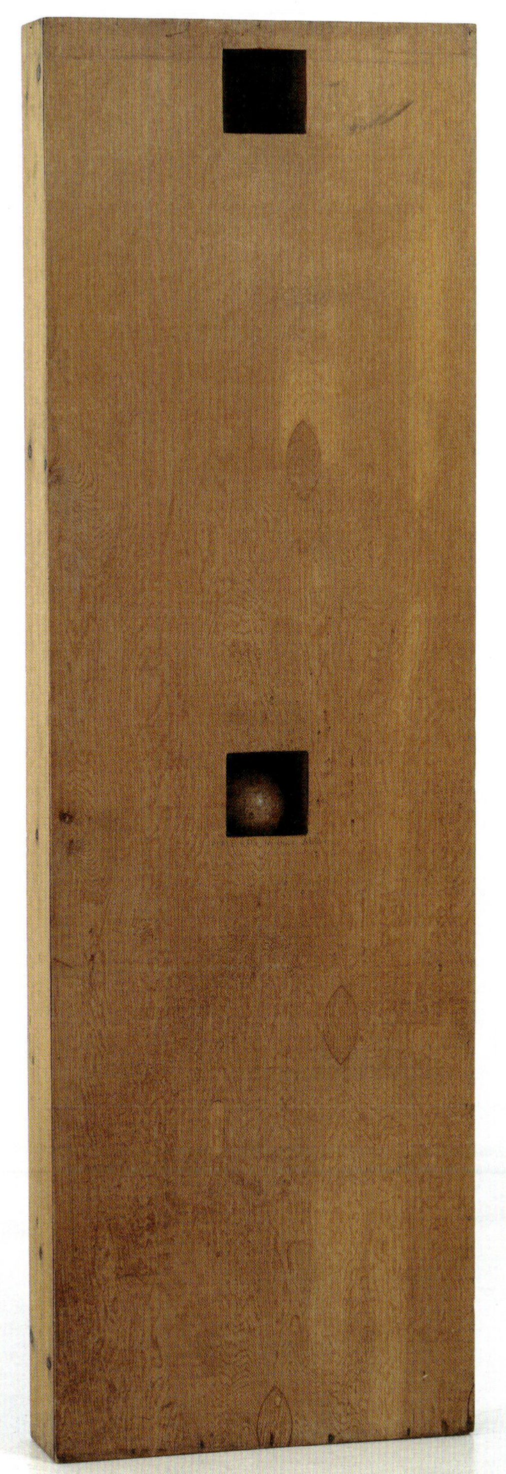

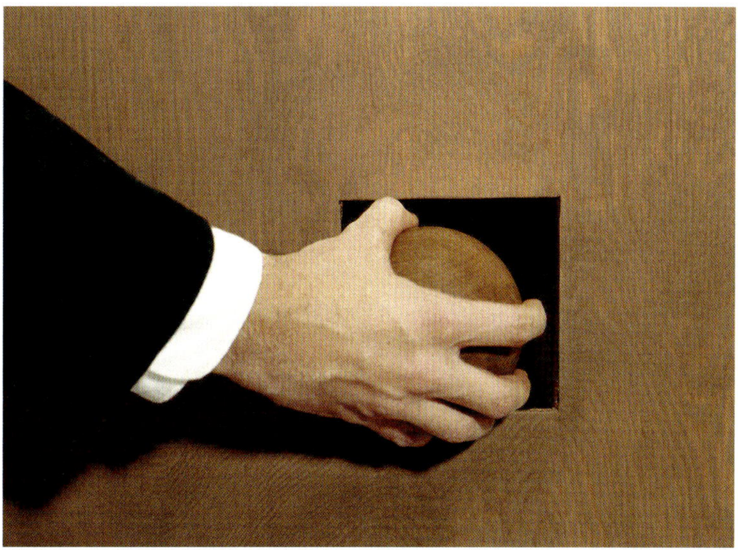

Fig. 2. Walter De Maria, *Ball Drop*, 1961–1964.
Plywood box and solid wood ball, box: 76 x 24 x 6¼ in.
(193 x 61 x 15.9 cm); ball: 4 in. (10.2 cm) diam.
Inscribed in pencil: "PLACE BALL IN HOLE ABOVE"
The Menil Collection, Houston

Fig. 3. Detail of Walter De Maria demonstrating
Ball Drop in his studio, c. 1964

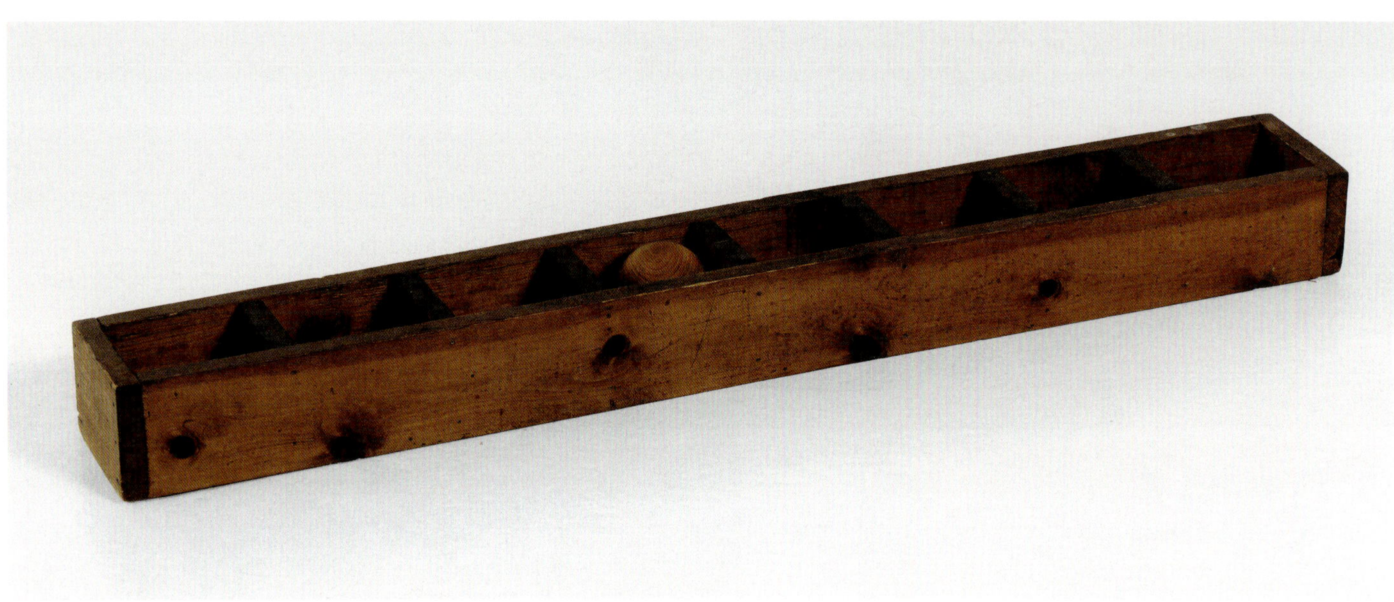

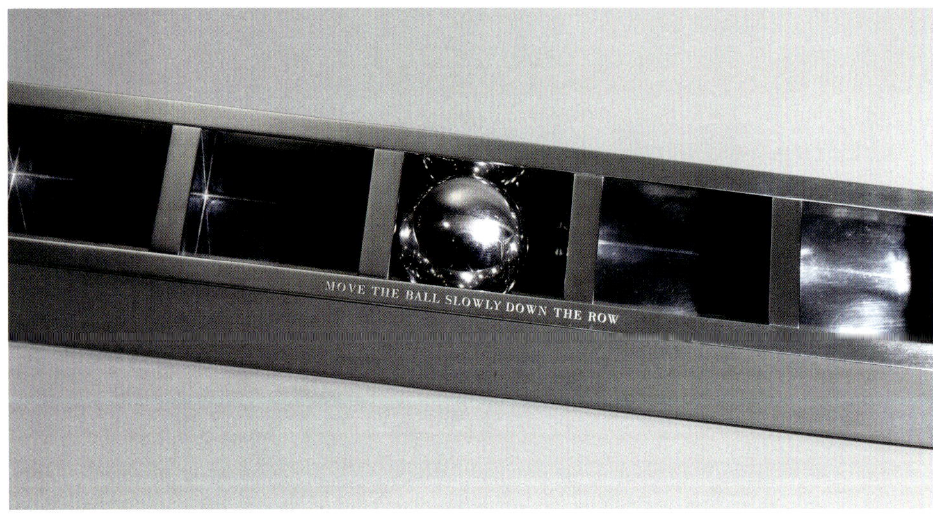

Fig. 4. Walter De Maria, *Move the Ball Slowly Down the Row*, 1962. Wood and graphite, box: 3⅝ x 5¼ x 42 in. (9.2 x 13.3 x 106.7 cm); ball: 4 in. (10.2 cm) diam. Inscribed in pencil: "MOVE THE BALL SLOWLY DOWN THE ROW" The Menil Collection, Houston

Fig. 5. Walter De Maria, *Move the Ball Slowly Down the Row*, 1962. Stainless steel with stainless steel ball, channel with eight compartments: 3⅝ x 5¼ x 42 in. (9.2 x 13.3 x 106.7 cm); ball: 4⅜ in. (11.1 cm) diam. Inscribed: "MOVE THE BALL SLOWLY DOWN THE ROW" Private collection

crack of the ball against the frame underscoring the blunt facticity and anti-illusionism of the work.

A related sculpture that deals with sound and time is *Move the Ball Slowly Down the Row*. First made in wood in 1962 (fig. 4) and later refabricated in stainless steel in 1965 (fig. 5), the work takes the form of a forty-two-inch channel divided into eight chambers. Inside the channel is a steel ball that can be moved incrementally "down the row" from chamber to chamber. Key to its interpretation is the instruction "slowly" in the title. In his formative 1968 article about the artist, David Bourdon writes that De Maria stressed the work's durational element in order to propose that the concept of time is malleable: "It can be your conception of slowness of any duration. One's choice enters in. You might move it in a minute, or every day, or every four months. It can be spread out over a year or years. Time can be stretched more than most people think."[12] The work not only has an aural component in the sound of the ball hitting the frame; it is also like a musical instrument to be played according to De Maria's instructions. The bars that divide the sculpture are analogous to the bars (or measures) that structure a musical score, denoting segments of time that may vary from one performance to another.

Ball Drop and *Move the Ball Slowly Down the Row* both inform De Maria's sound sculpture *Instrument for La Monte Young* of 1965–1966 (figs. 6 and 7), a narrow open container made of aluminum in which sits a solid aluminum ball. Integrated into the sculpture are three contact microphones that in theory could be connected to an amplifying system.[13] The built-in mics and mixer pick up and amplify any ding created as the ball is rolled inside the channel. The amplification is not used for its own sake but to emphasize the sculpture's characteristics and material. By design, movement of the ball is limited. Essentially, it can be rolled at variable speeds from left to right and right to left, with some opportunity for up and down. As a result, the area available for movement restricts the sound activity, reducing it to a minimum, with a high possibility for repetition. The distinctive thing about this instrument is that the process of rolling the ball is both the subject and source of the music. What you see is what you hear. Both *Instrument for La Monte Young* and *Move the Ball Slowly Down the Row* provoke the viewer by way of a contradiction. On the one hand, because the works lack formal complexity they allow for quick assessment and comprehension of the sculptural form. But on the other hand, the practically infinite arrangement and rearrangements possible in *Move the Ball Slowly Down the Row* and the endless rolling movements and acoustic responses conceivable in *Instrument for La Monte Young* open both works to temporal limitlessness.[14]

Along with these acoustic sculptures, De Maria made two sound recordings during the 1960s: *Cricket Music* (1964) and *Ocean Music* (1968) (see pp. 24–25).[15] The *Cricket Music* piece begins with a drum roll lasting one minute forty-eight seconds, followed by a six-second pause, and then a 6/8 drum loop lead. This type of loop has an Afro-Cuban feel that offers the listener a few different ways to hear the rhythm. The cymbal pattern strongly suggests feeling the rhythm in 6, but the dotted 8th notes that are played on the bass drum, toms, and snare drum imply a 4 feel. This style is popular in drum music originating in West Africa as well as in the larger African diaspora from Cuba to New Orleans. Prominent throughout are the alternating sounds of the high and low tom, which almost dominate the recording until the addition of the chirping crickets at around eleven minutes. In contrast with the later *Ocean Music*, the drum loop noticeably evolves in *Cricket Music*. At around sixteen minutes, audible changes to the toms occur. It is difficult to tell if

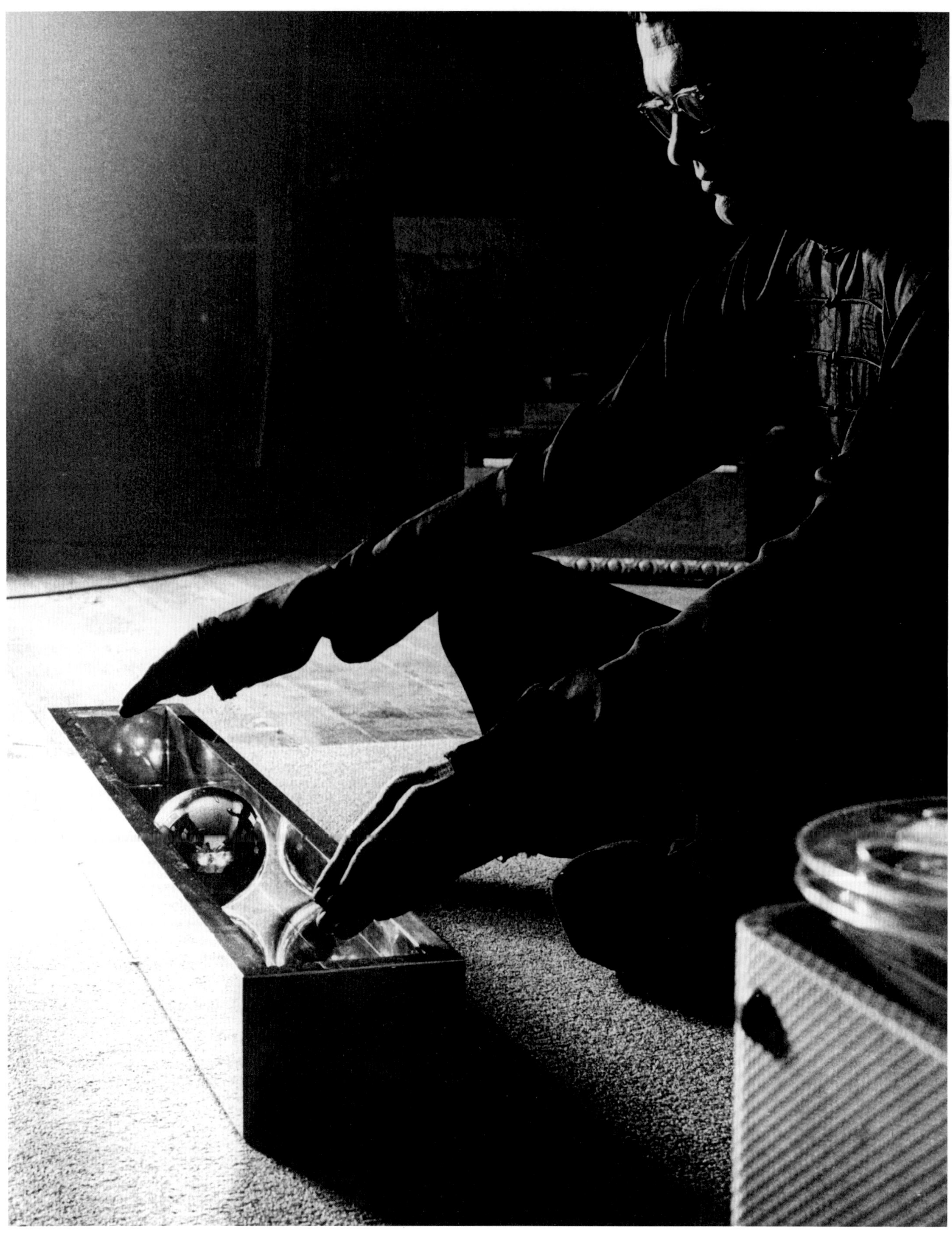

Fig. 6. La Monte Young performing Walter De Maria's *Instrument for La Monte Young*, 1966.
Aluminum with contact microphone, 3¾ x 36 x 5¼ in. (9 x 91.5 x 13 cm). Inscribed: "INSTRUMENT
FOR LA MONTE YOUNG Number [ ] of 9 copyright © WALTER DE MARIA & LA MONTE YOUNG
1966" Private collection

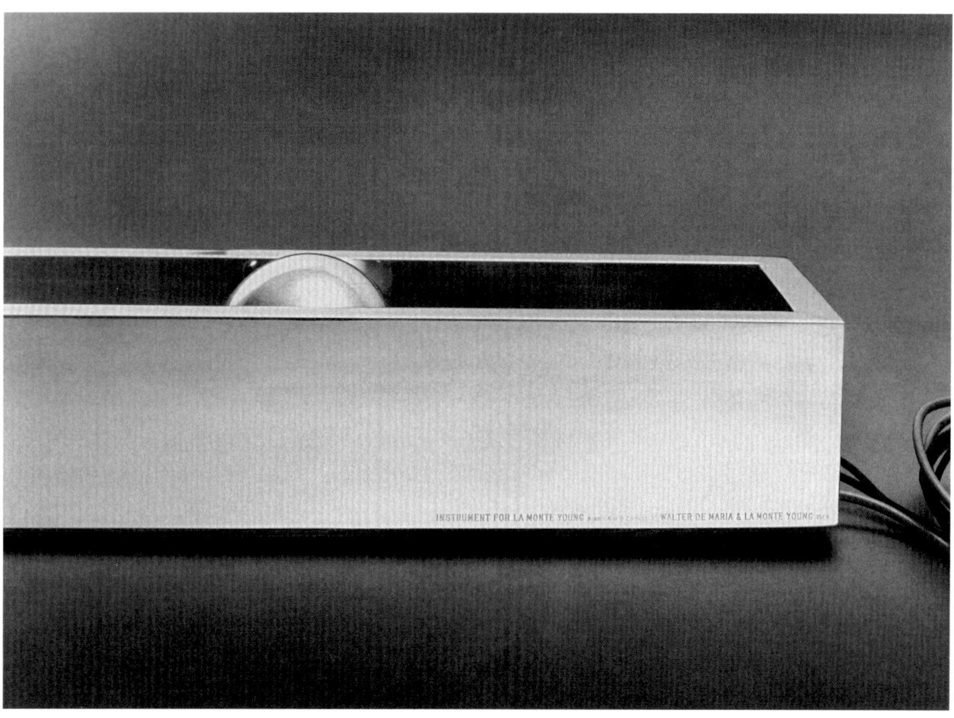

Fig. 7. Detail, Walter De Maria, *Instrument for La Monte Young*, 1966

this is a result of the intense work involved in sustaining the virtuoso drumming performance by De Maria or an application of a technique that became known as phasing, which experimental composers used in the mid-1960s. Whatever the case, over the next few minutes, a varying emphasis on the bass drum affects the cymbal patterns, and the rhythm changes to a quarter-note, eighth-note, quarter-note, eighth-note loop, making it slightly squarer. These shifts introduce layers of intricacy and subtlety to the score. Then each element of the drum parts fades out to afford the piece a final section. The tom parts fade first over the course of a minute or so, followed by the snare drum. The bass drum fades last, leaving only the cymbal. The cymbal pattern shifts in the last few minutes, making a slightly longer loop before it, too, eventually fades.

The most unexpected audio element of *Cricket Music* definitely is that of a low-flying propeller airplane, which can be heard prominently from minutes twenty to twenty-two and subtly thereafter until the work's close. The surprise introduction of the airplane prompts the listener's mind to move from earth to sky. In its concluding minutes *Cricket Music* introduces the concepts of vast spatial distances—between insect and airplane—and wave frequencies, both audible and inaudible, which are being transmitted from the earth at all times to infinite points in space. It positions the work within the new environmentalism of the 1960s, a movement that was emerging concurrently from a radical critique of government and an acknowledgment of ties among ethical, environmental, and social issues. For De Maria, these ideas stem from *Cricket Music* to reach their apex in his land work.

There may also be a more pointed reference in the sound of the airplane and the style of drumming in *Cricket Music*. In October 1962, a U.S. surveillance plane discovered the presence of Soviet missiles in Cuba—one of the first occasions that the recently established National Photographic Interpretation Center publicly interpreted images it obtained for the government by aircraft. High-altitude spy planes could produce evidence of ballistic missile facilities by collecting signals and imagery using radio waves alongside other intelligence sensors. This aerial surveillance of the land triggered the Cuban Missile Crisis, which brought the world to the brink of nuclear war. It is conceivable that the worldwide tension created during the thirteen-day scare informed the unexpected presence of the airplane in the final minutes of *Cricket Music*. This aerial perspective on the land would later become key to imagining—and imaging—De Maria's expansive works of Land Art.

Like *Cricket Music, Ocean Music* combines two basic compositional elements: an acoustic drum kit and a prerecorded sound drawn from nature, in this case surface waves breaking across an ocean. In both pieces, these prerecorded loops are used to create repetitive, rhythmic musical patterns and a dense layer of sound over the drummed acoustic element performed by De Maria. Of the two, *Ocean Music* relies on a purer process. Eight minutes of unaccompanied sounds of crashing waves open the piece. Gradually, the sound of the drums builds to meet and challenge the soothing sound of the waves. De Maria plays a single 4/4 drum loop inflected with a rock style, using only bass drum, snare drum, and ride cymbal, which crescendos around the second half of the work. The drum loop, played for more than ten minutes, draws us in and forces us to be alert, sensitive to each detail of the performance. Subtle changes in the way the snare drum is played or the amount of resonance a cymbal builds up come to be monumental. For the duration of the track the sounds—played or field-recorded—collide at more or less equal levels; but the overtones of the drumming begin to regulate the inherent randomness of the waves as they naturally differ in height, duration, and shape on each audible break. De Maria's drumming superimposes a certain order over the physics that govern the unpredictable movements of the ocean. In this sense, the composition relates to the artist's best-known attempt to harness nature as a sculptural component in his long-term installation *The Lightning Field* (fig. 8). This work of art in western New Mexico attempts to connect sky and earth by way of a gridded field measuring one mile by one kilometer and containing four hundred sharpened metal spikes that are, in effect, lightning rods intended to solicit the energy of lightning. Famously, the work is pictured attracting lightning in four of the six photographs De Maria selected, including the cover, to illustrate *The Lightning Field* as part of its unveiling in the April 1980 issue of *Artforum*.

Ocean Music communicates De Maria's interest in energy systems—sound, wave, and, as *The Lightning Field* demonstrates, electrical—while signposting his growing disillusionment with chance-based procedures in music. His questioning of chance, whether as a strategy or as a subject of investigation, continued with *Statue of John Cage* (fig. 9), a critical portrait of the creative impact that composer John Cage had in the 1960s. While Cage himself was openly critical of musical Minimalism, his adopting principle of being in the moment gave him a philosophical framework that drove his automatic techniques and linked him with Minimalism in both art and music. It is probably more accurate to say that he prefigured Minimalism in music the same way that Barnett Newman's work anticipated Minimalism in painting. In any case, Cage was undoubtedly a model for artists and composers. The key strategies De Maria shared with Cage's musical practice were his use of raw materials drawn from everyday life and his roots in the observation of nature and of processes that happen independently of a composer's conscious control, such as an ocean wave or a chirping cricket.

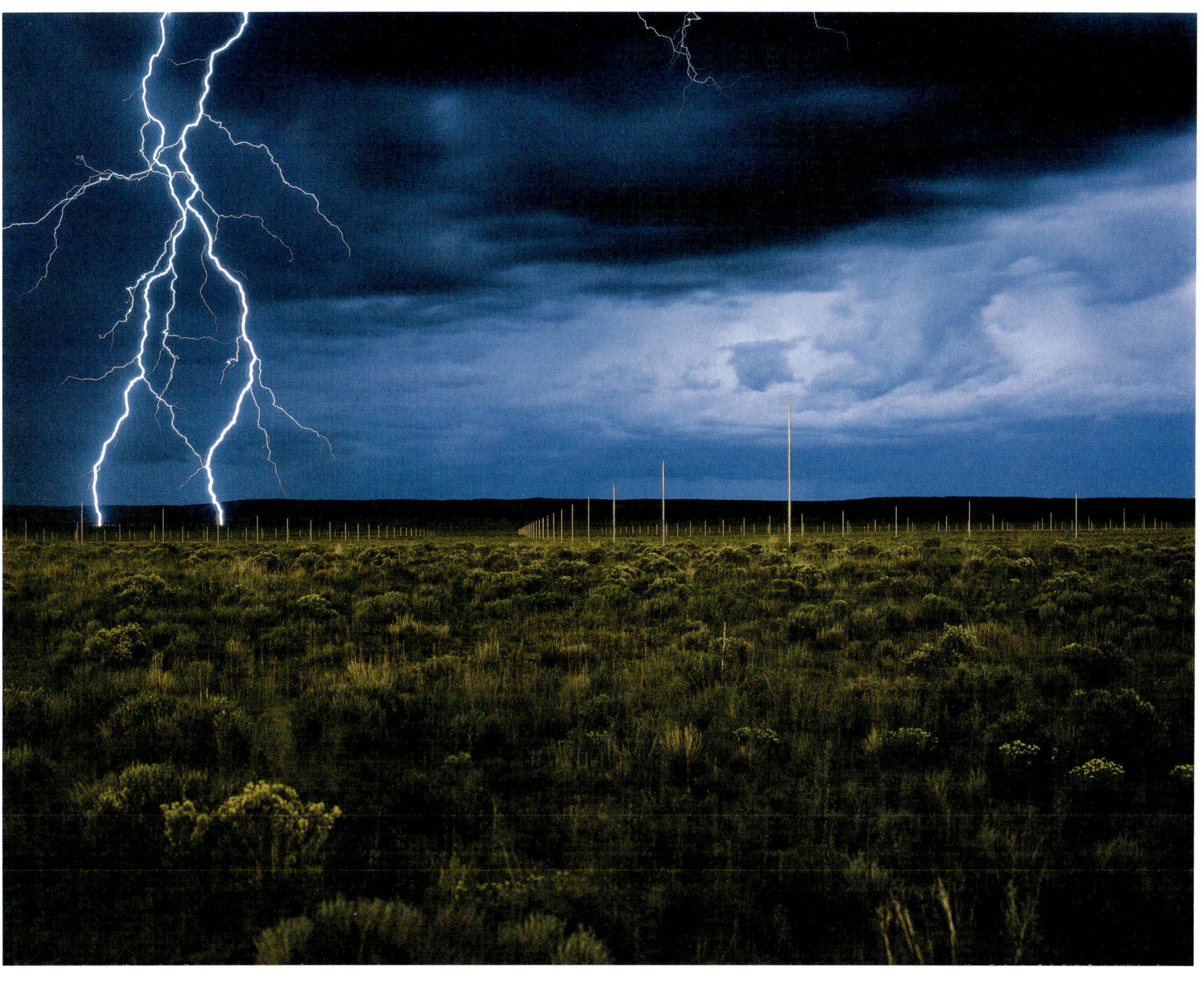

Fig. 8. Walter De Maria, *The Lightning Field,* 1977. 400 stainless steel poles spaced 220 ft. (67 m) apart; average height: 20 ft. 6½ in. (6.3 m); overall: 1 mi. x 1 km. Long-term installation, western New Mexico. Commissioned and maintained by the Dia Art Foundation, New York

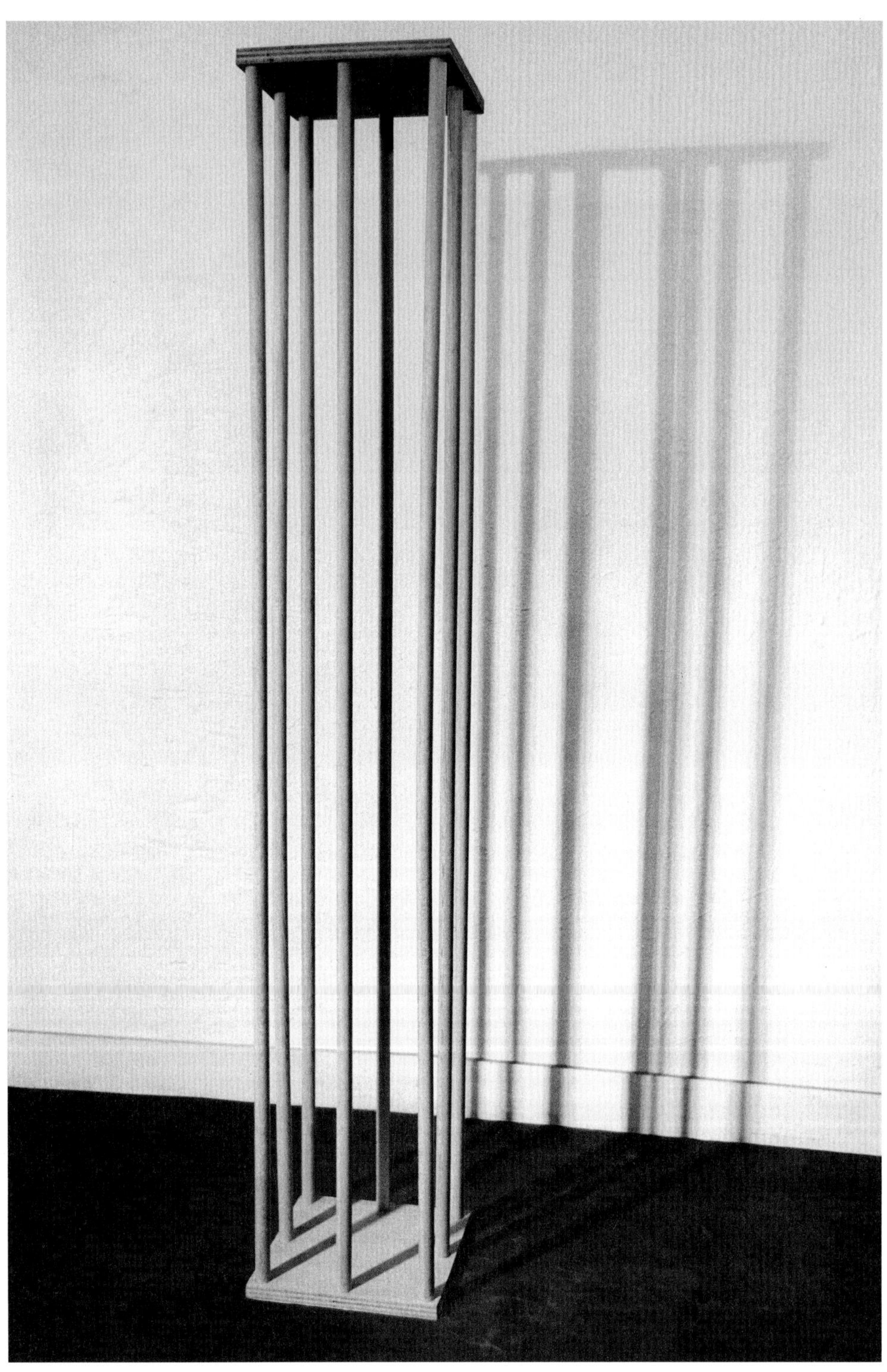

Fig. 9. Archival photograph of Walter De Maria's original version of *Statue of John Cage*, created in 1962. Wood, 85 x 14½ x 14½ in. (215.9 x 36.8 x 36.8 cm). It was subsequently destroyed by the artist and then reconstructed in 1984. The new version of the sculpture was acquired by the Menil Collection in 2015.

De Maria's portrait does not represent Cage in any traditional sense, such as physical likeness, but as a tall, narrow, self-supporting cage constructed of plywood and wooden rods. Before its unveiling, De Maria sent Cage the following note:

> Dear John Cage,
> I think that it is only fair that I tell you that I have made a statue of you. Like the other sculptures and boxes that I am showing in this show, the sculpture was made about a year ago. It is 7 feet one inches tall. I do hope that this does not offend you.
>
> Should you not be able to see the show, I am enclosing a photo of the statue, which I would like you to keep.[16]

Kathleen Merrill Campagnolo describes the work in this way:

> A visual pun, the tall, narrow structure *Statue of John Cage* suggests a standing human form. But, larger than life-size, . . . the sculpture was impos-ing. The column-like cage stood directly on the floor. Unlike most statues, it was not on a pedestal, but approachable on the same level as the viewer. However, with no visible doors or hinges, there was no way in or out of the cage; the structure was a closed system. De Maria's sculpture of Cage implies a contradiction: accessible yet inaccessible.[17]

De Maria destroyed the original *Statue of John Cage*, although it was recon-structed in 1984. Two subsequent graphic representations— *Portrait of John Cage* and *Portrait of the School of Cage, Caged* (fig. 10), both from 1962—and two 1965 stainless steel versions titled *Cage* and *Cage II* (figs. 11 and 12) still exist.[18] The works on paper offer an additional clue to De Maria's conflicting feelings of admira-tion for and condemnation of Cage's influence at that time. He views Cage's musical disciples as trapped in a prison cell:

> Cage was interested in all the freer forms of modern music. . . . I was sympa-thetic to him. . . . Later when I was to start reflecting the ideas of chance, I became less and less interested in Cage. . . . When I made my statue of John Cage, I think it was partly a recognition of the fact that Cage may have been caging a lot of people.[19]

While his *Instrument for La Monte Young* functioned as a kind of homage to the composer, De Maria's portraits of Cage are more ambivalent. With these works, he enters into dialogue with the avant-garde music of his time as an informed critic rather than a naive devotee.

In this essay I have argued that De Maria's interest in music was integral to the development of his artistic practice during the 1960s. His early sculptures often have an acoustic element to them or function as "instruments" to be played according to De Maria's instructions. By referencing composers such as Young and Cage in his work, De Maria indicated his own—often overlooked—place in the downtown avant-garde while intervening in the critical discourse surrounding what would come to be known as Minimalist music. With his own recordings *Cricket Music* and *Ocean Music*, De Maria produced percussive soundscapes that prefig-ure the Land Art for which he would become known. Rather than representing nature in any sentimental sense, these compositions conjure humankind's surveil-lance of and control over the landscape and its inhabitants, their rhythmical repeats systematically mapping the earth, sky, and sea.

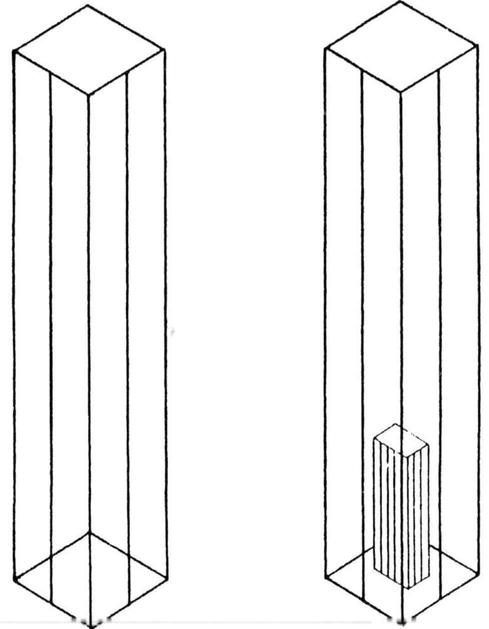

Fig. 10. Walter De Maria, *Portrait of John Cage*, 1962, and *Portrait of the School of Cage, Caged,*
1962. Graphic drawing. Published in *Fluxus cc V TRE* (Fluxus Newspaper No. 2), New York:
Fluxus, February 1964, p. 4

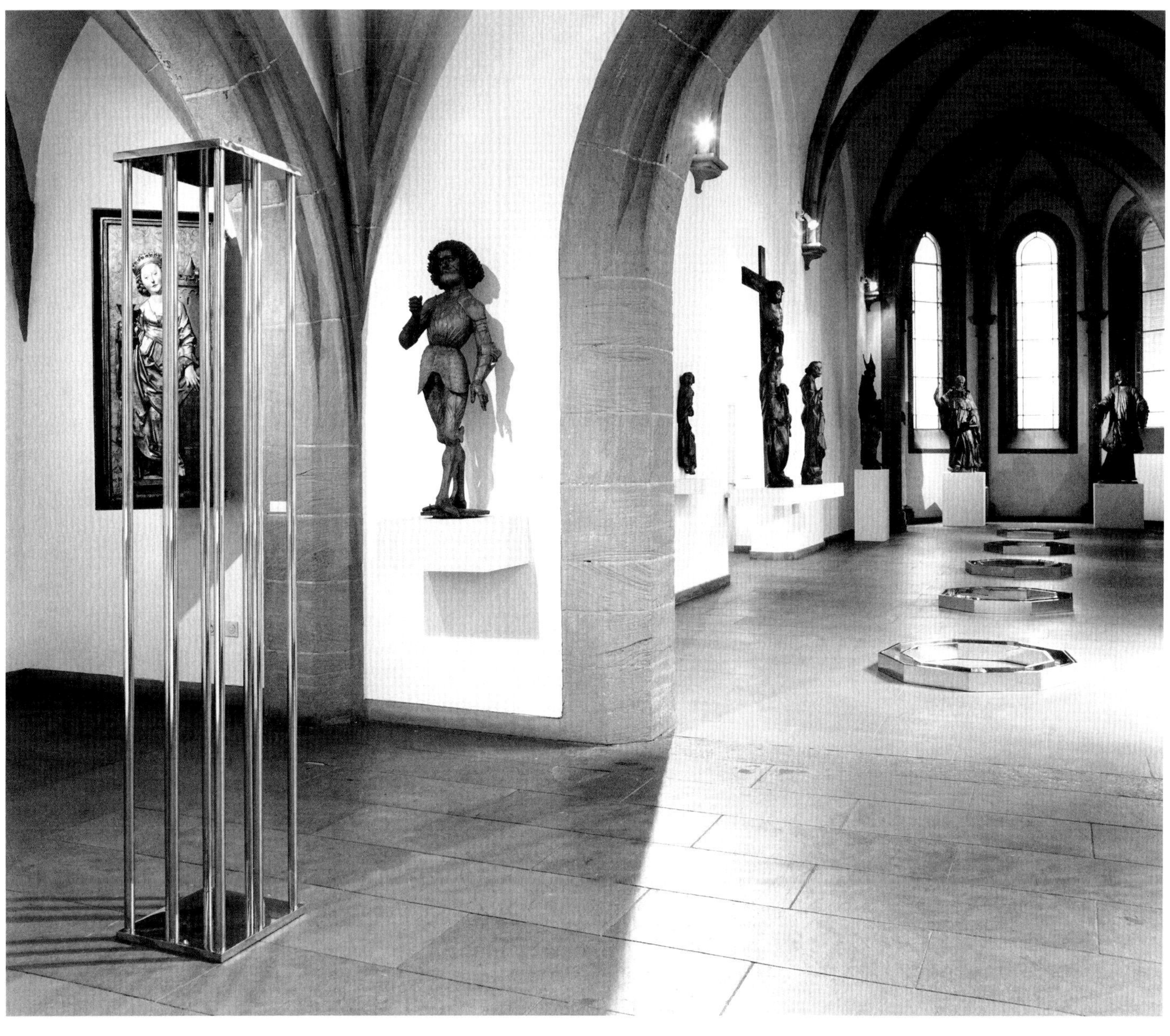

Fig. 11. Installation view of *Walter De Maria: Der Grosse Erdraum, 8 Skulpturen, 44 Zeichnungen,* *(Large Earth Room, 8 Sculptures, 44 Drawings)*, Hessisches Landesmuseum Darmstadt, May 31–July 28, 1974. Left: *Cage*, 1965, Edition 1/2. Stainless steel, 85 x 14½ x 14½ in. (215.9 x 36.8 x 36.8 cm). Right: *5–9 Series* (1973–1974)

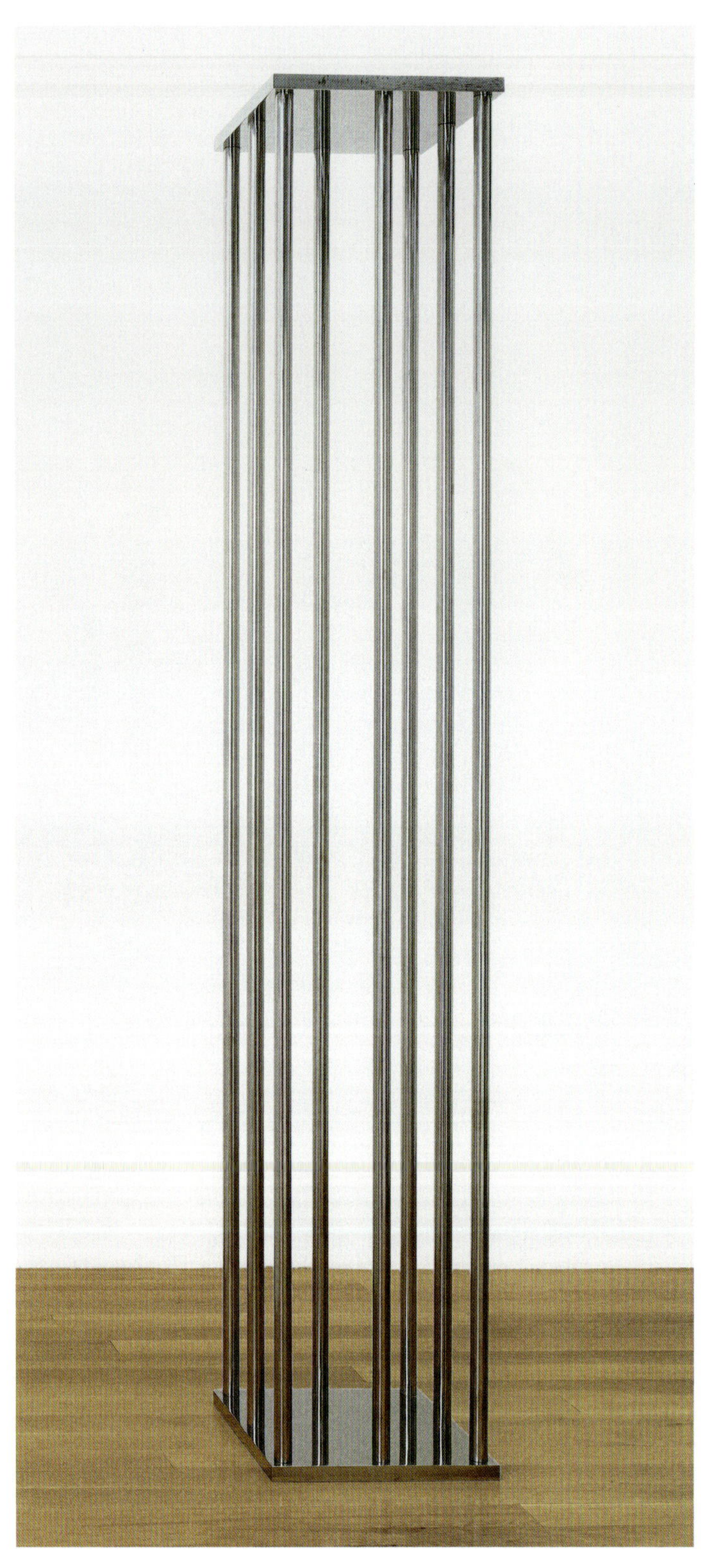

Fig. 12. Walter De Maria, *Cage II*, 1965, Edition 2/2. Stainless steel, 85 x 14½ x 14½ in. (215.9 x 36.8 x 36.8 cm). The Museum of Modern Art, New York, Gift of Agnes Gund and Lily Auchincloss

Sources and Notes

1. Oral history interview with Walter De Maria, October 4, 1972, Archives of American Art, Smithsonian Institution.

2. Oral history interview with Dennis Oppenheim, July–August 1995, Archives of American Art, Smithsonian Institution.

3. The application of the term "Minimal" for musical rationales was introduced in the United States by critic and composer Tom Johnson in 1972 but only fully acknowledged after his influential *Village Voice* essay of 1977, "What Is Minimalism Really About?" (reprinted in Johnson, *The Voice of New Music* [Paris: Editions 75, 1989], n.p. www.editions75.com/books/thevoiceofnewmusic.pdf). Johnson embraced the term "Minimalism" to describe his compositions, which were often based on mathematical and systematized processes in an attempt to make them as clear as possible. He employed words like "repetition," "tiny variations," and hyper-clarity" with the aim of "encouraging more subtle perceptions."

4. Keith Potter, *Four Musical Minimalists* (Cambridge: Cambridge University Press, 2000), 35.

5. Young's "Collaboration Event: to" concerts were held on May 2 and May 6, 1960.

6. Oral history interview with Walter De Maria.

7. Better known is De Maria's role as drummer with the group The Primitives, which included Lou Reed, John Cale, and Tony Conrad. The Primitives experience fused the partnership between Cale and Reed that would become The Velvet Underground.

8. Gerard Forde, "Plus or Minus 1961: A Chronology 1959–1963," in *Plus or Minus 1961: Founding the Expanded Arts,* ed. Julia Robinson and Christian Xatrec, 50–67. www.academia.edu/4061715/_Plus_or_Minus_1961_A_Chronology_1959–1963.

9. *New Grove Dictionary of American Music,* "La Monte Young," by David Farneth, vol. 4, 579, quoted in Potter, *Four Musical Minimalists*, 348.

10. Oral history interview with Walter De Maria, 19.

11. Edward Strickland, *Minimalism: Origins* (Bloomington and Indianapolis: Indiana University Press, 1993), 262.

12. David Bourdon, "Walter De Maria: The Singular Experience," *Art International* 12, no. 10 (December 1968): 40.

13. The lot description for the work at auction on May 14, 2009, was *"Instrument for LaMonte Young,* stamped with the artist's signature, title, number and date 'INSTRUMENT FOR LAMONTE YOUNG NUMBER 2 OF 9 COPYRIGHT WALTER DE MARIA & LAMONTE YOUNG 1966' (lower edge) solid aluminum with three contact microphones; Eurorack MX 602A amplifier equalizer 3½ x 36 x 5 in. (8.8 x 91.4 x 12.7 cm) Executed in 1966. This work is number two from an edition of nine."

14. Barbara Haskell highlighted the connection between Young and De Maria in her 1984 publication that accompanied the Whitney Museum of Art exhibition *Blam! The Explosion of Pop, Minimalism, and Performance 1958–1964*: "The bare simplicity and lack of even a literary component imbued these plywood rectangles with a monumentality analogous to Young's musical compositions in which single notes were sustained for long durations without expressive variation of pitch or rhythm" (99).

15. Recordings of *Cricket Music* and *Ocean Music* are available at: www.ubu.com/sound/demaria.html.

16. De Maria, letter to John Cage, January 2, 1963, quoted in Richard Kostelanetz, *John Cage*, ed. Richard Kostelanetz. (London: Allen Lane, 1974), pl. 51, and in Kathleen Merrill Campagnolo, "In the Company of Cultural Provocateurs: Radical Portraiture in the 1960s," in *This Is a Portrait If I Say So: Identity in American Art, 1912 to Today*, Anne Collins Goodyear, Jonathan Frederick Walz, and Kathleen Merrill Campagnolo, eds. (New Haven and London: Bowdoin College Museum of Art in association with Yale University Press, 2016), 71.

17. Kathleen Merrill Campagnolo, "In the Company of Cultural Provocateurs," 71.

18. Two editions of *Cage* exist: *Cage*, 1965, MMK Museum für Moderne Kunst, Frankfurt am Main, and *Cage II*, 1965, Museum of Modern Art, New York.

19. Oral history interview with Walter De Maria.

Jane Porter McFadden's dissertation "Practices of Site: Walter De Maria and Robert Morris, 1960–1977" (University of Texas at Austin, 2004) considers the early and interdisciplinary practices of these two artists and their association with the emergence of Fluxus and minimalist music.

Kathleen Merrill Campagnolo's master's thesis "Walter De Maria: Art and Homage, 1960–1972" (Courtauld Institute of Art, 2009) is an excellent read that explores certain under-recognized aspects of De Maria's practice, his influence within the cultural context in which the works were made, and how key early works lay the foundations for his mature style.

Molleen Theodore examines the breadth and complexity of De Maria's work—his writing, statements, painting, sculpture, music, film, land work, photography projects, and installation design, including a section on La Monte Young—in her dissertation "Beyond 'Meaningless Work': The Art of Walter De Maria, 1960–1977" (City University of New York, 2010).

The author would like to thank composer and percussionist Jason Treuting for transcribing Walter De Maria's *Cricket Music* (1964) and *Ocean Music* (1968). These transcriptions provided invaluable inspiration for this essay.

Cricket Music and *Ocean Music*: Notated Scores

Transcribed by Jason Treuting

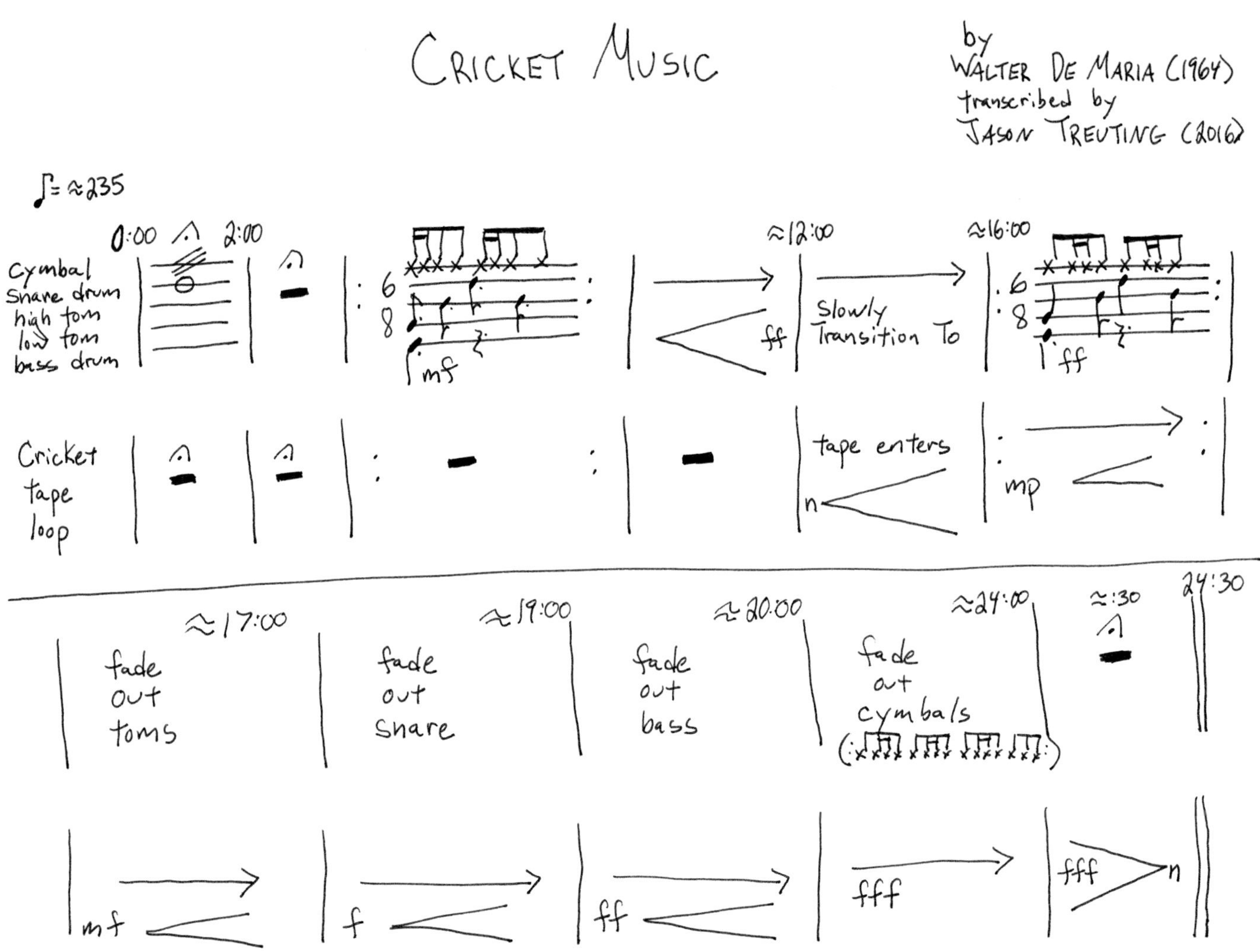

Ocean Music

by
WALTER DE MARIA (1968)
transcribed by
JASON TREUTING (2016)

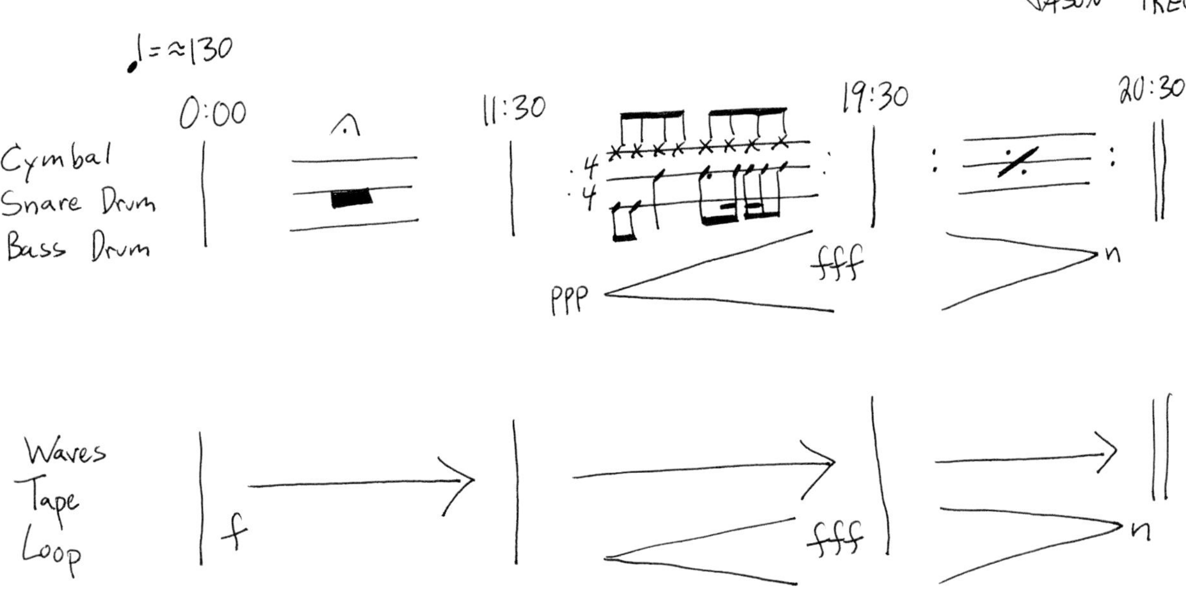

Superimpositions
Caitlin Haskell

Walter De Maria's art asks a viewer to hold in mind a few ideas at once. If you've ever had the pleasure of experiencing his works in person, you may reasonably feel that my estimation of "a few" is a considerable understatement. There are exactly two thousand plaster rods, for example, within the ten-by-fifty-meter field of *The 2000 Sculpture* (fig. 13). Likewise, there are no fewer than four hundred stainless steel poles dispersed throughout the one-mile-by-one-kilometer parcel of land and sky in New Mexico that constitutes *The Lightning Field* (fig. 14). The former artwork is a dense matrix, thick with white forms, that feels resistant to physical penetration—a protection communicated both by the artist's stated wishes, which instruct visitors to observe it from a short distance away, and also by the work's perceptible resistance to intrusion into its tightly patterned expanse. The latter artwork, by contrast, is airy and subtly alive, with a porous boundary that allows beholders to experience it from within. Yet each, in its different way, denies an all-at-once encounter with the artwork, placing at stake a viewer's sense that he or she can comprehend it fully. These works don't demand the same sort of slow and practiced looking that one might imagine necessary to appreciate a gallery of European paintings, but it takes time to come to know them. Any familiarity with their material realization occurs gradually and synthetically, as a patchwork of incomplete observations stitched together and regularly checked against one's beliefs about the artwork as a whole.

Contending with compositions executed at such superhuman scale would seem to demand a heightened coordination of mental and sensory activities, and yet De Maria's works tend to emphasize the thresholds where these faculties cease to align and begin to falter. It is a matter of human biology, for instance, that the largest of his artworks surpass the limit of our perceptual capacities, even though they remain fathomable to our minds. In practical terms, this disjunction makes it possible to refer to two sets of dimensions, which exist simultaneously but are not coextensive. The first-person parameters of the artwork (what we sense) tend to be dwarfed by what the artist defines as its objective borders—that is to say, what we read about it on a statistics sheet or find in the dimensions field of an identifying label.[1] Because these two systems of measure and two ways of knowing the world are so drastically out of sync, it encourages a sort of toggling back and forth between the abstract idea of the artwork and our sensory knowledge of it. Having recognized this disparity, it is less important to determine which of these systems is primary than it is to acknowledge their coexistence as complementary and mutually enhancing experiences of the artwork. Oscillation between them is encouraged.

Among De Maria's commentators, Lars Nittve in particular has underscored the artist's proclivity for "drawing attention to the gap between experience and fact," to the unpredictability of the world around us and to the comparative tidiness of the intellectual abstractions developed to manage its instability.[2] This gap is readily

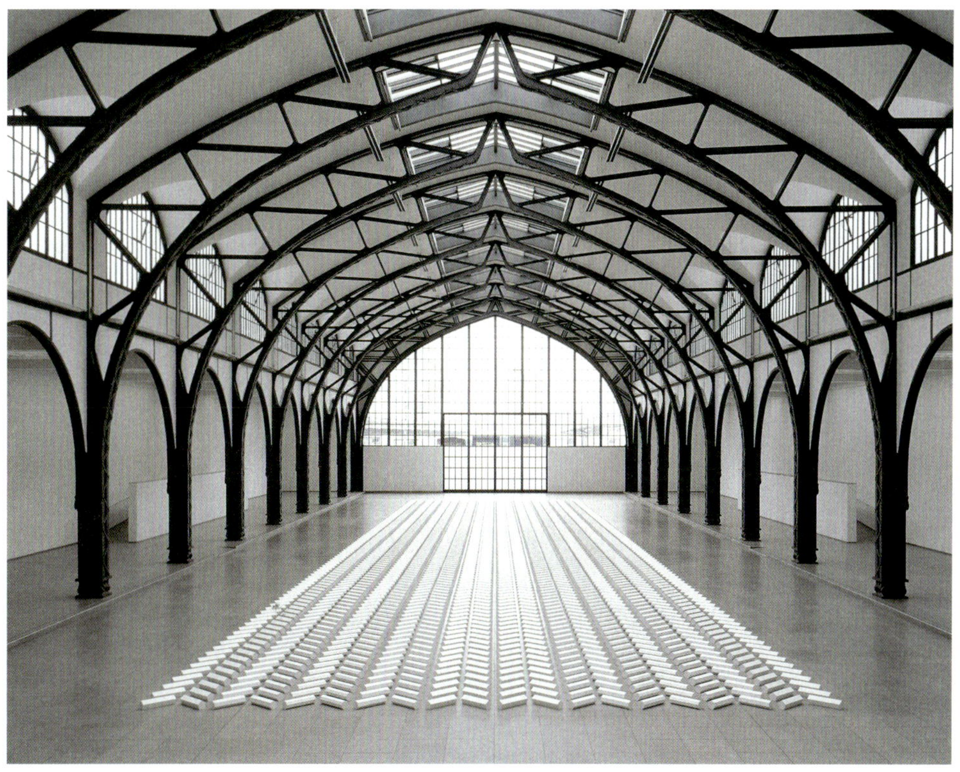

Fig. 13. Walter De Maria, *The 2000 Sculpture*, 1992. 2,000 solid plaster rods shaped in the form of 5-, 7-, and 9-sided polygons, each 1⅝ ft. (1/2 m) long: 800 5-sided rods, each 4¾ in. (12 cm) diam., 800 7-sided rods, each 4⅝ in. (11.9 cm) diam., 400 9-sided rods, each 4⅝ in. (11.8 cm) diam.; entire sculpture: 32¾ ft. x 164 ft. x 30½ in. (10 m x 50 m x 12 cm). Collection Walter A. Bechtler Foundation, Switzerland

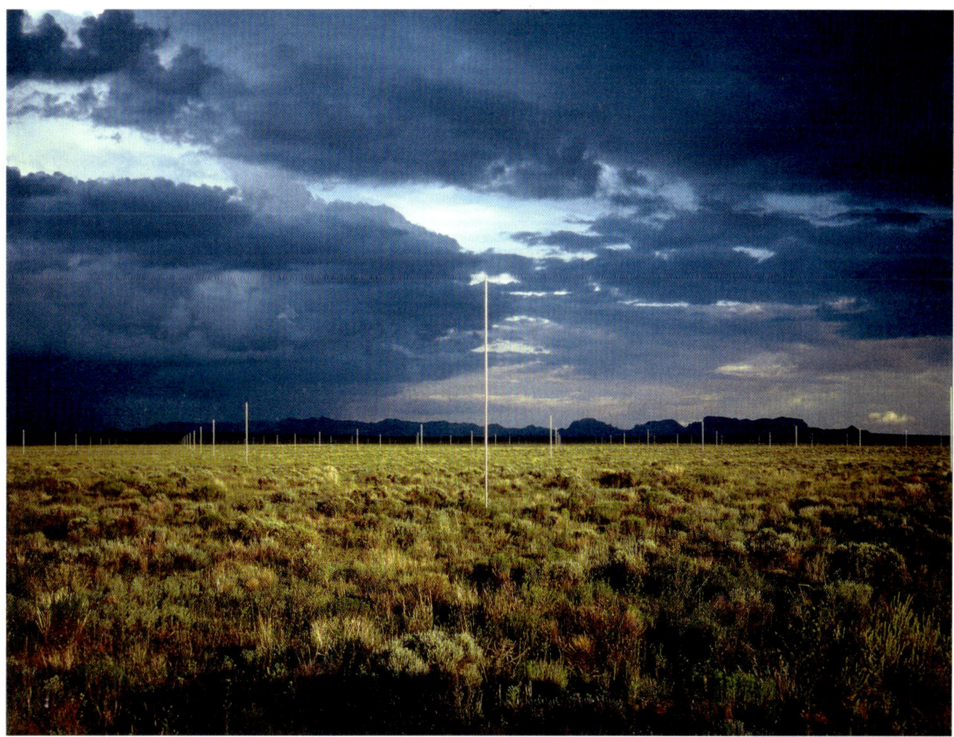

Fig. 14. Walter De Maria, *The Lightning Field,* 1977. 400 stainless steel poles spaced 220 ft. (67 m) apart; average height: 20 ft. 6½ in. (6.3 m); overall: 1 mi. x 1 km. Long-term installation, western New Mexico. Commissioned and maintained by the Dia Art Foundation, New York

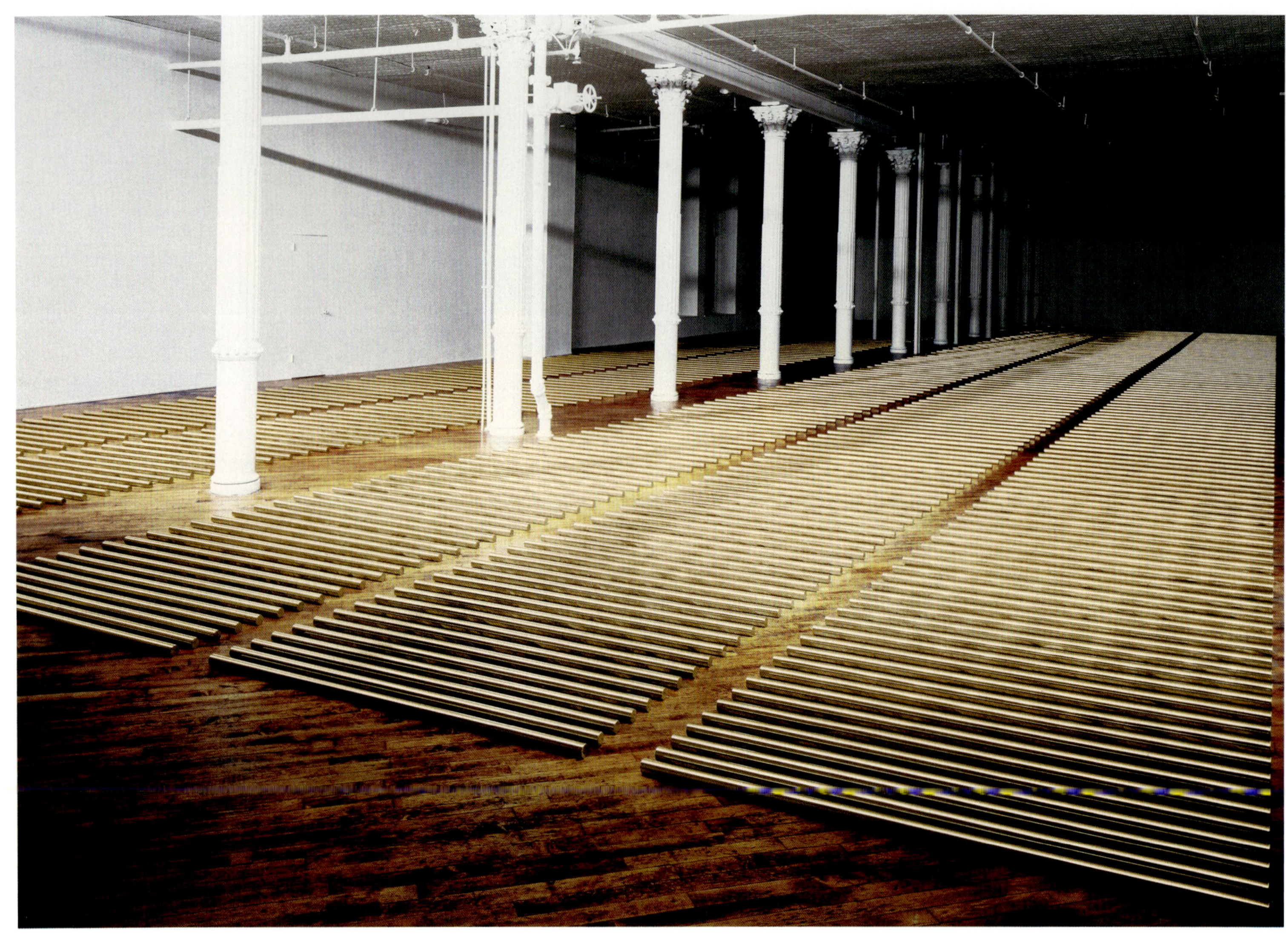

Fig. 15. Walter De Maria, *The Broken Kilometer*, 1979. 500 brass rods, each 2 in. diam. x 6 ft. 6¾ in. (5.1 cm diam. x 2 m); overall: 45 x 125 ft. (13.7 x 38.1 m). Long-term installation, 393 West Broadway, New York. Commissioned and maintained by the Dia Art Foundation, New York

apparent in De Maria's earthworks and his most physically imposing indoor installations, yet the artist's more modestly scaled pieces also have the power to bring empirical certainty to heel.

While viewing the handmade multiple known as the *Pure Polygon Series* (1975–1976), for instance, I recently felt my own ability to synchronize identification and numeration, pointing and counting, simply slip away. The artwork consists of seven individual drawings of polygons, each presented on a large sheet measuring thirty-six inches square and rendered in graphite lines so faint it would be futile to try to reproduce them here. Gazing at the nonagon, I started to count its sides, saying the numbers to myself as my eyes followed a clockwise path. Yet by the time I reached the fifth side, near the bottom of the sheet, it occurred to me that I had lost sight of where I began. My starting point, on the opposite side of the form, was by now out of view. I would try again and see if I could make my way around the nine-part itinerary, but as before, I lost my footing turning the fourth corner. If it hadn't been so pleasant to waver in this way, recognizing that De Maria had anticipated this cognitive/perceptual slippage, I might have fought harder to resist the loss of control.

A similarly humbling phenomenon can happen in the presence of *The Broken Kilometer* (fig. 15), a large-scale indoor installation in SoHo comprising five hundred two-meter-long brass rods. Standing before the artwork, there is a temptation to start counting—to test the eyes and know firsthand how many of the gleaming rods you can individuate before they begin to read as a homogenous yellow-metal mass. For me, the count can rise to about forty before I start to lose trust in my vision. Little more than a third of the distance down the row, I have already found my breaking point—a natural limit reached well within the artwork's stated boundaries.

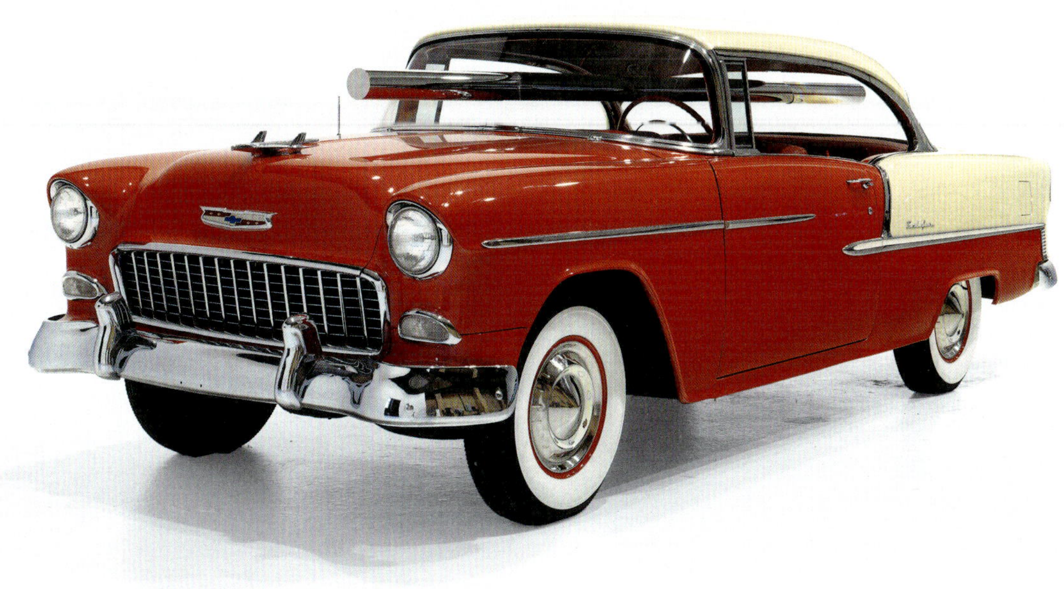

Fig. 16. Walter De Maria, *Bel Air Trilogy: Circle Rod*, 2000–2011. Stainless steel rod with 1955 Chevrolet Bel Air two-tone hardtop, rod: 4 in. diam. x 12 ft. (10.2 cm diam. x 3.7 m); automobile: 5 x 16 x 6 ft. (1.5 x 4.9 x 1.8 m). Collezione Prada, Milan

At Least Ten Meanings

"Every good work of art," De Maria remarked in 1974, "should have at least ten meanings." Even if it "seem[s] to have no more than two or three meanings. . . . That's far short of being a successful work."[3] How De Maria managed to concentrate so many meanings—or perhaps more accurately, how he created so many situations that would allow meaning to proliferate—is well worth considering. I have suggested already that he does this in part by overwhelming his viewer with such a variety of ways to conceive of his artworks that it erodes one's certainty in making basic pronouncements about them. Through a considered use of multiple frames of reference that together produce affirming and contradictory views of the artwork, De Maria brings a viewer to doubt his or her conviction that things are what they claim to be. At times, the superimposition of these frameworks might create the impression that a surplus of information is reaching us, while at others they might read as a blockage obstructing our perception of the artwork.

Culture conditions us to believe that an object has a single identity. Already in his early career, however, De Maria was looking for ways to challenge this expectation. In 1962, just two years after he moved from Berkeley to New York, he proposed the *Three-Continent Project: Square in U.S. desert, Horizontal Line in the Sahara, Vertical Line in India*, an artwork that would draw together vastly disparate geographies and superimpose these distinct fields of information. "Three continents are needed for this image," he wrote, and "when all of the lines are photographed from the air, [and] the photos are placed one on top of the other, the image will reveal a cross in a square."[4] This is among the clearest examples of De Maria creating simultaneity through coextensive systems that overlap as images but don't line up conceptually. Quite literally, the satellite photographs were intended to be viewed as superimposed images, their perfect registration challenging a viewer's

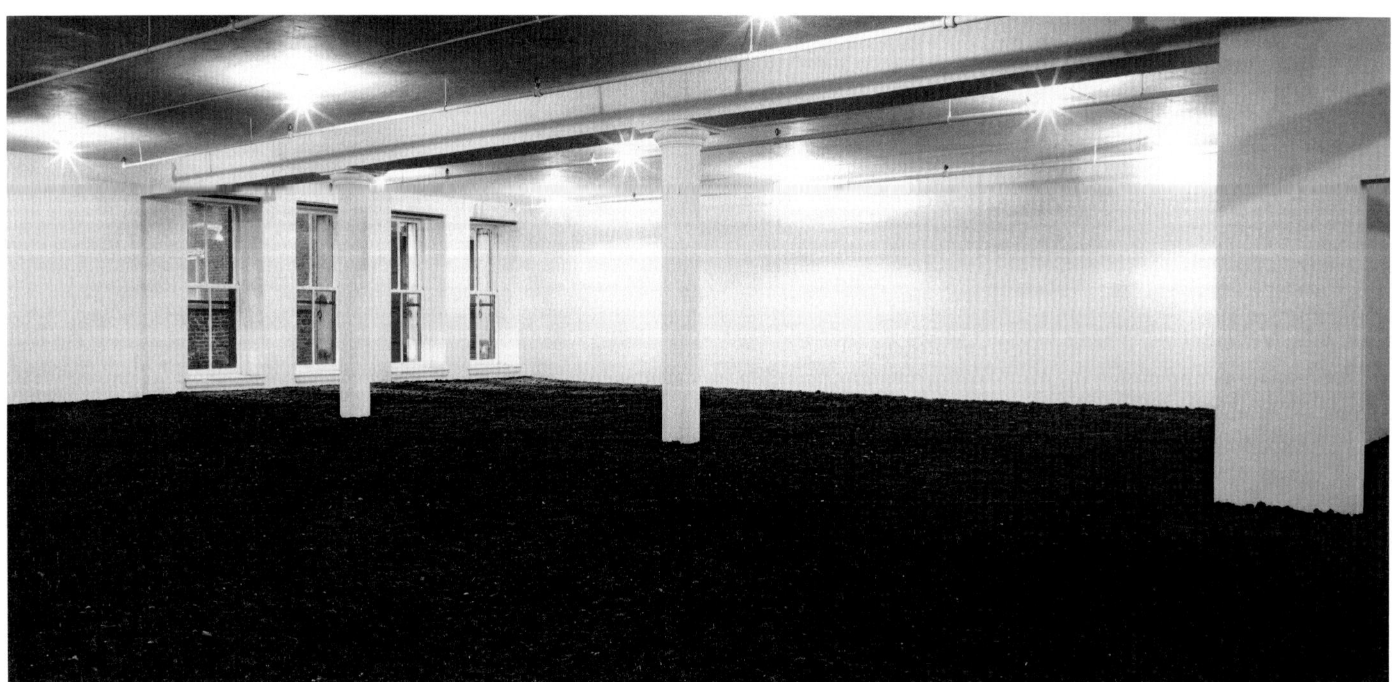

Fig. 17. Walter De Maria, *The New York Earth Room*, 1977. Earth, peat, and bark covering an area of 3,600 sq. ft. (335 sq. m) and piled 22 in. (56 cm) deep. Long-term installation at 141 Wooster Street, New York. Commissioned and maintained by the Dia Art Foundation, New York

knowledge that India, North Africa, and the American Southwest are land masses that will never touch and cannot be viewed together at once. One might think of it as a Land artwork in which the earth's topography could exist in greater concentration than its does in lived experience, three hundred parts per hundred.

The tripartite nature of *Three-Continent Project*, which already points to the artist's interests in multiplicity and simultaneity, forms something of a bookend in De Maria's career with one of his most astounding late works, *Bel Air Trilogy: Circle Rod* (fig. 16). Here the artist's rhetoric of precision, honed over decades and capable of producing structures of archetypal clarity, takes on a playful tone. The artwork brings together two ideas that can be held together in the mind's eye but that took years of work to fabricate with the seamless precision for which De Maria's art is known. There is little difficulty seeing these two things together at once, as car and as rod, and also in their combined state of car-and-rod. But, like miles and kilometers, or two hundred fifty cubic yards of earth and the New York apartment that holds it (fig. 17), the two refuse to mix.

As a matter of chance, when *Bel Air Trilogy* was on view at the Menil Collection in the fall of 2011, René Magritte's painting *The Listening Room* (*La chambre d'écoute*) (fig. 18) happened to be hanging in an adjacent gallery.[5] The timing was coincidence, but it is hard to imagine two artworks that articulate with greater clarity the cognitive unease we feel when contending with competing frames of reference. Magritte's green apple and the room that (barely) contains it are equally fictitious, and neither element, taken on its own terms, would present any special challenge to our understanding. But by forcing us to take both together, the image presents a productive frustration of the type we encounter physically, in the round, in works such as De Maria's *Large Red Sphere* (fig. 19). Viewed in reproduction, the sculpture and the building that holds it are a cognate of Magritte's painting, which like-

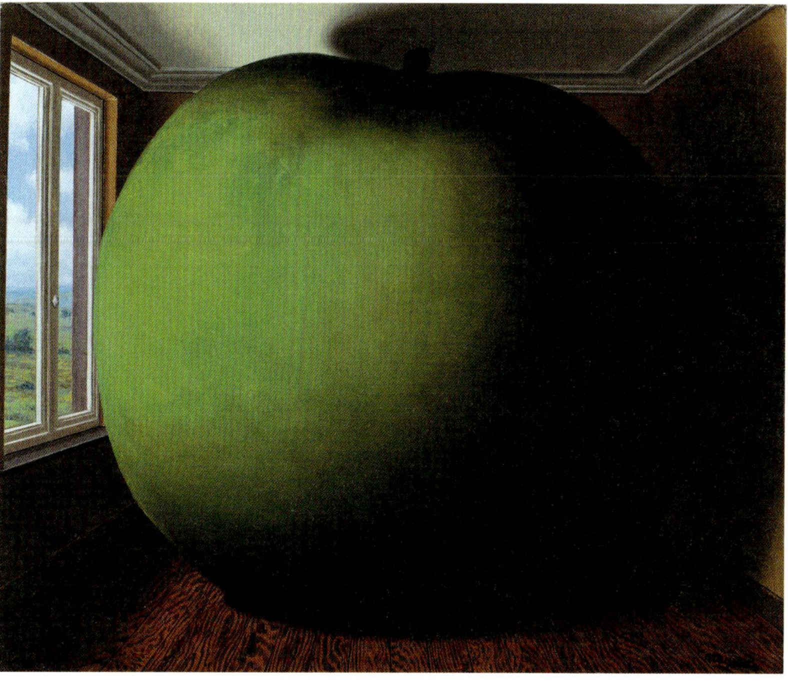

Fig. 18. René Magritte, *The Listening Room (La chambre d'écoute)*, 1952. Oil on canvas, 17¾ × 21¾ in. (45.2 × 55.2 cm). The Menil Collection, Houston, Gift of Fariha Friedrich

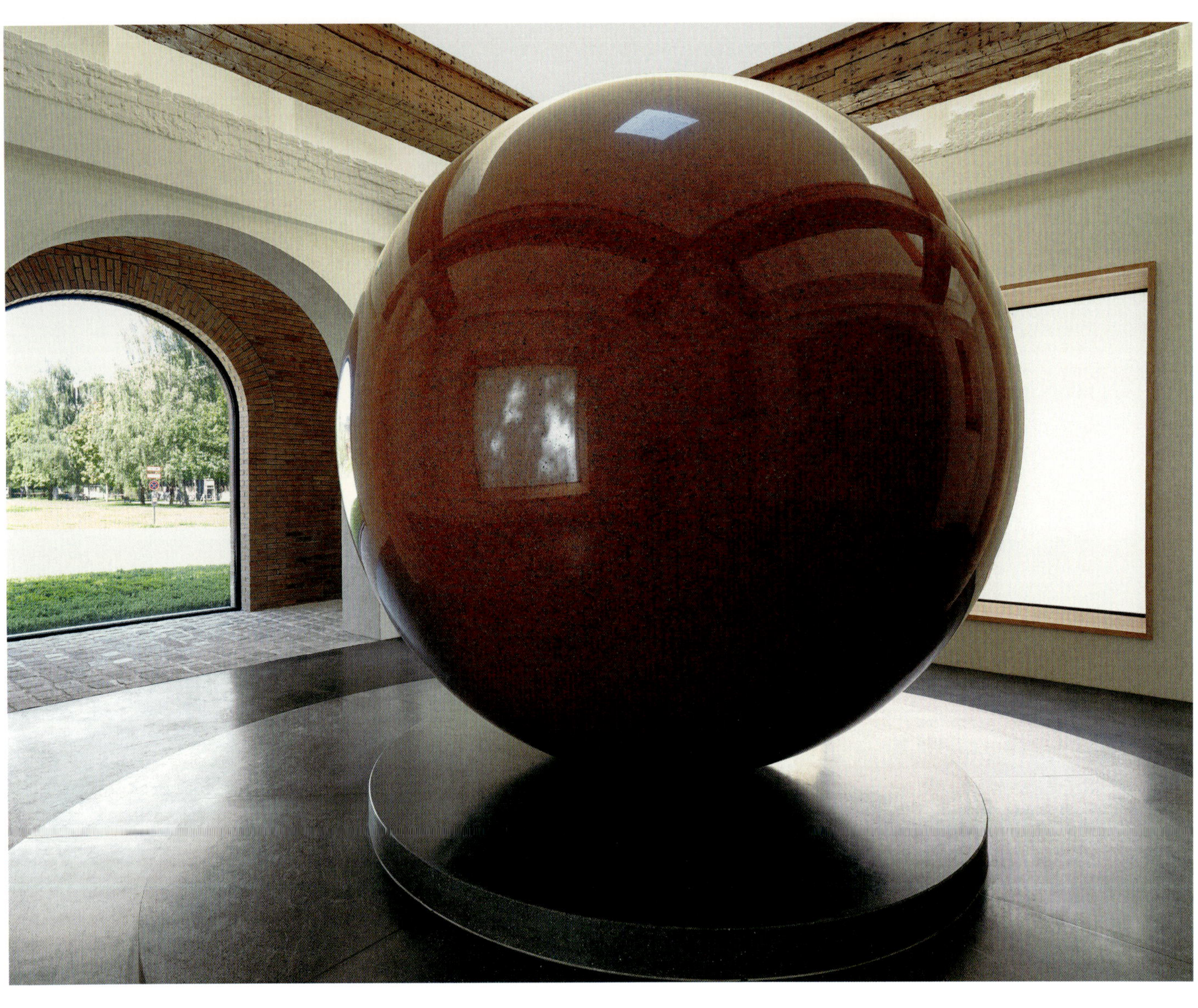

Fig. 19. Walter De Maria, *Large Red Sphere*, 2010. Granite, 102 in. (259 cm) diam., 25 tons. Türkentor, Kunstareal Munich. Maintained by Pinakothek der Moderne and Museum Brandhorst

wise denies a totalizing view through the swelling of a single form placed squarely within a constrictive architectural frame. But I hesitate to draw the analogy too closely, or to limit the meaning of *Large Red Sphere* to that of obstruction. Indeed, the title of a related work on the island of Naoshima, *Seen/Unseen Known/Unknown* (fig. 20), might illuminate the ends to which such a strategy would be employed.

Having never visited Naoshima, I have to take the word of Yuji Akimoto, the commissioning curator, who characterized De Maria's approach as that of a research scientist. And yet if this is so, the artist was an inquirer as concerned with blindness as he was with insight. "He examines the site, takes careful measurements," Akimoto explains, and still the space is uncertain and indeterminate. "It is difficult to know where to stand. . . . The boundary between the inside and the outside is ambiguous. . . . It gives rise to a feeling of insecurity."[6] Despite the binary structure of the title, the experience of the artwork impresses on a viewer that seeing and knowing are not categorical conditions, but rather states along a continuum. For every disclosure it allows, there is an attendant obstruction to offset it, causing one's sense of how much is seen and known to rise and fall. Again, oscillation is encouraged.

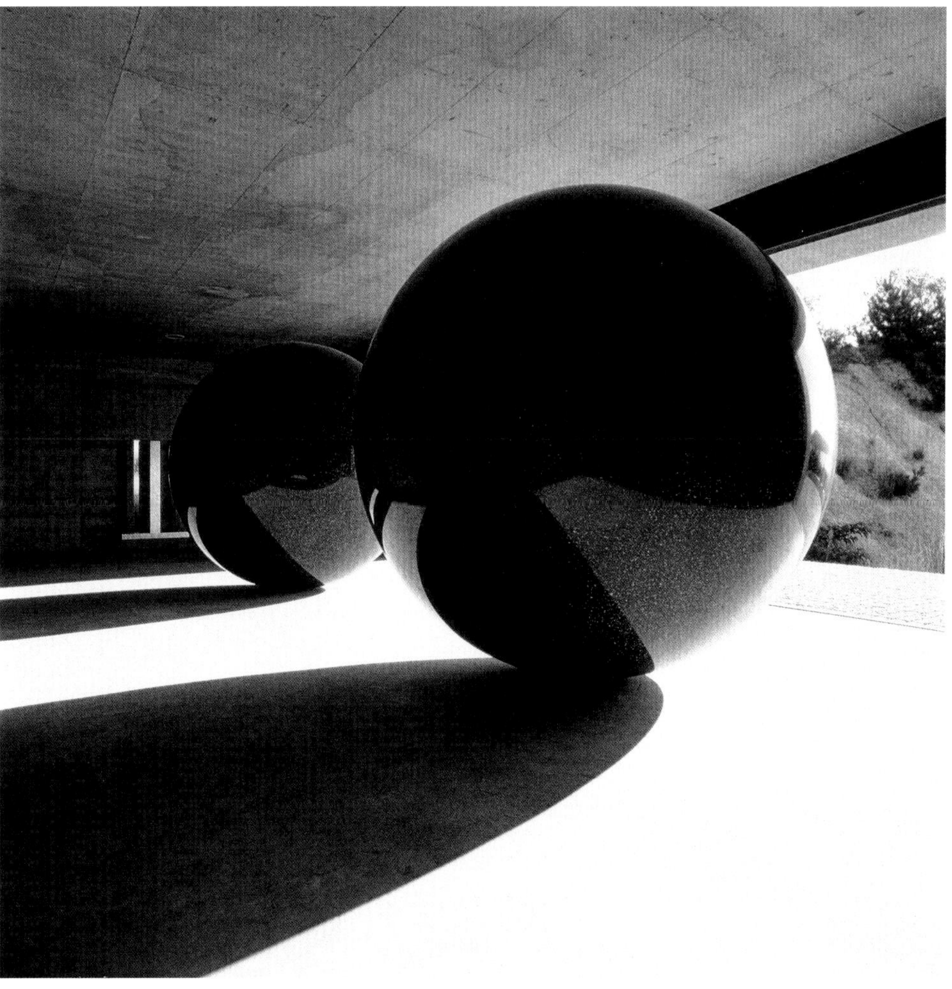

Fig. 20. Walter De Maria, *Seen/Unseen Known/Unknown*, 2000. Granite, mahogany, gold leaf, and cement, two granite spheres, each 72½ in. (184.2 cm) diam., 9 tons; two wooden sculptures with gold leaf, each 34⅝ x 10⅝ x 52¾ in. (88.1 x 27 x 134 cm); two cement pedestals, each 39⅜ x 15 x 5⅛ in. (100 x 38 x 13 cm). Naoshima Contemporary Art Museum, Seaside Gallery (designed by Tadao Ando)

In Eight or Nine Parts

In "The Lightning Field: Some Facts, Notes, Data, Information, Statistics, and Statements," De Maria writes that due to the angle of the sun at certain times of day, "70 to 90 percent of the poles become virtually invisible."[7] That is, of the four hundred highly polished stainless steel poles, as few as forty might appear. By now we know to resist the finality of factual claims like this. Since the loss occurs optically, not absolutely, a first question might be: "Virtually invisible from where?" There are, however, instances in De Maria's oeuvre when the removal of a component is not contingent on weather conditions or where a viewer stands, but rather is stipulated in the work's installation instructions.

A case in point is *Large Rod Series: Circle/Rectangle 5, 7, 9, 11, 13* (figs. 21–29). It confounded me, when first learning about this sculpture, that it is sometimes presented as a configuration of nine rods and at other times as a configuration of eight.[8] The nine-rod presentations can take one of two rectangular forms, elongated or compact, while the eight-rod presentation takes the form of a circle, with pieces radiating outward, like the spokes of a wheel. In a work of so few discrete parts, all of which can fit comfortably within one's field of vision, losing one-ninth or gaining one-eighth, as the case may be, is a change of such magnitude that it should be obvious to a beholder. And yet the artwork in no way feels less complete or less complex in the circular arrangement than it does in its rectangular variations.

On the high plains of Catron County, New Mexico, we are perhaps better prepared to see less than a whole artwork, or to understand "the whole" as a shifting and variable entity to which we will never have complete access. Inevitably, there will be poles that we cannot see—either because they are behind us, or too far away, or because the sun is high and shining brightly, or because a bird has suddenly caught our attention, or an irregular patch in the land has caused us to drop our eyes and mind our footing. This is all to say that there is more going on within the total artwork than we can attend to. "The sum of the facts," indeed, "does not constitute the work or determine its esthetics."[9]

Taken alone, the absence of one pentagonal rod in the circular presentation of *Large Rod Series: Circle/Rectangle 5, 7, 9, 11, 13* might seem like an aberration—a quirk that makes this indoor artwork less predictable than the well-grounded floor sculptures of earlier Minimal art. But an omission of such consequence gives teeth to the notion that this artwork has three equally valid identities and ensures that the circle and rectangle displays are not understood as merely decorative differentiations. The quantitative change in the number of rods guarantees De Maria's ideal of an artwork that can never be presented comprehensively, all at once, in all its parts. The qualitative result is that when the circle is present, the rectangle cannot be.[10] Of course, it's nearly there, for those who are aware of it—implied, really, through the symmetry of the numerical series and just within the imagination's reach. But for it to exist in the mind's eye, the viewer must supply a missing material component.

A defining quality of De Maria's art is its resistance to exclusive definitions. Building artworks as if by stacking and superimposing frameworks that don't fully align, he starts his viewer down a path of mutually reinforcing and contradicting understandings of his art: as an idea formulated in language, as a physical structure, and as an imaginative image that may or may not be available to bodily experience. The revelation of *Large Rod Series: Circle/Rectangle 5, 7, 9, 11, 13* comes when eight rods, as opposed to nine, are not felt primarily as a loss of material—be that one sculptural element, one hundred twenty pounds of total weight, or four fewer facets and two fewer end plates to reflect light—but rather as an increase of the sculpture's potential realizations. In De Maria's typically paradoxical way, one rod's removal might result in an expanded understanding of the artwork. He asks us to hold this possibility in mind.

Notes

1. See, for example, Walter De Maria, "The Lightning Field: Some Facts, Notes, Data, Information, Statistics, and Statements," *Artforum* 18, no. 8 (April 1980): 58, as well as the pamphlets produced for long-term installations such as *The Broken Kilometer* (1979) and *The New York Earth Room* (1977).
2. Lars Nittve, "The Sublime," in *Walter De Maria: The 5–7–9 Series* (New York: Gagosian Gallery, 1992), reprinted in *Walter De Maria: Sculptures* (Rome: Gagosian, 2012), 8. See also Nittve, "All Fives, Sevens, and Nines," *Artforum* 30, no. 10 (Summer 1992): 70–73.
3. Oral history interview with Walter De Maria, October 4, 1972, Archives of American Art, Smithsonian Institution. This statement will strike the ears of many as a departure from De Maria's advocacy of "meaningless work," however their sentiments converge.
4. Quoted in Lucy Lippard, *Six Years: The Dematerialization of the Art Object* (1973; repr. Berkeley: University of California Press, 1997), 55.
5. Confirmed by Clare Elliott, Associate Curator, The Menil Collection, e-mail message to author, April 8, 2016.
6. Yuji Akimoto, "Is There Harmonious Order in the Universe?" in *Walter De Maria: Seen/Unseen Known/ Unknown* (Okayama City: Naoshima Contemporary Art Museum, 2002), 40, 42.
7. De Maria, "The Lightning Field: Some Facts," 58.
8. As explained in *Walter De Maria: Large Rod Series: Circle/Rectangle, 1984–1986* (New York: Xavier Fourcade, 1986), 27, the sculpture was first created with two display possibilities: the eight-bar circle and the nine-bar short rectangle. The rectangle was exhibited first, in February 1986, and the circle followed in October 1986.
9. De Maria, "The Lightning Field: Some Facts," 58.
10. It is worth noting that De Maria never mandated alternation among the circle, short rectangle, and long rectangle configurations: "These transformations are completely optional. A work may remain forever in one form should this be decided." See *Walter De Maria: Large Rod Series: Circle/Rectangle, 1984–1986*, 27.

Large Rod Series: Circle/Rectangle 5, 7, 9, 11, 13, 1986

Large Rod Series: Circle/Rectangle 5, 7, 9, 11, 13, 1986. Edition 1/2. Stainless steel. Collection of
the Dallas Museum of Art through the TWO x TWO for AIDS and Art Fund and the San Francisco
Museum of Modern Art through the Phyllis C. Wattis Fund for Major Acquisitions

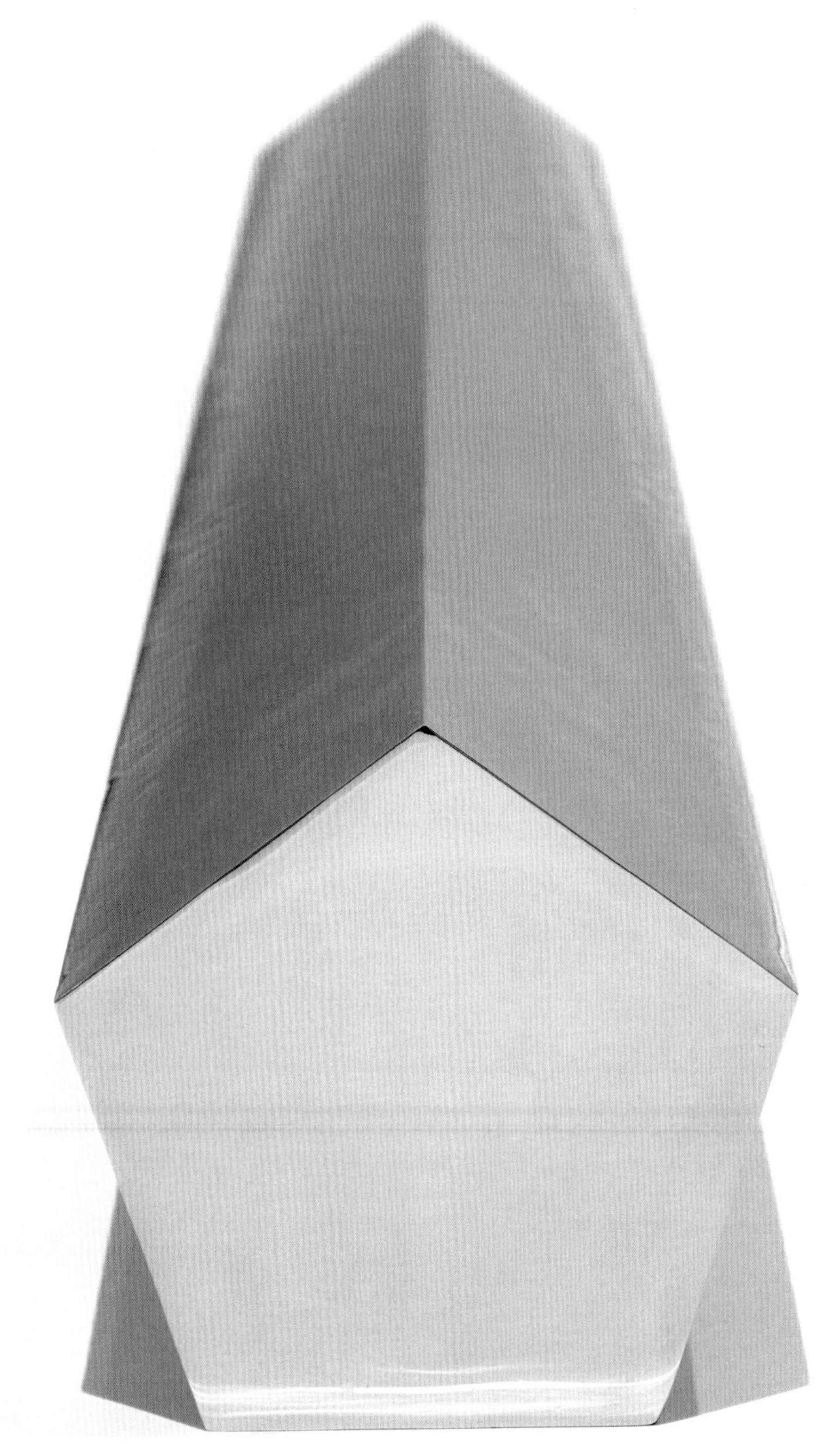

Fig. 21. Detail, 5-sided rod

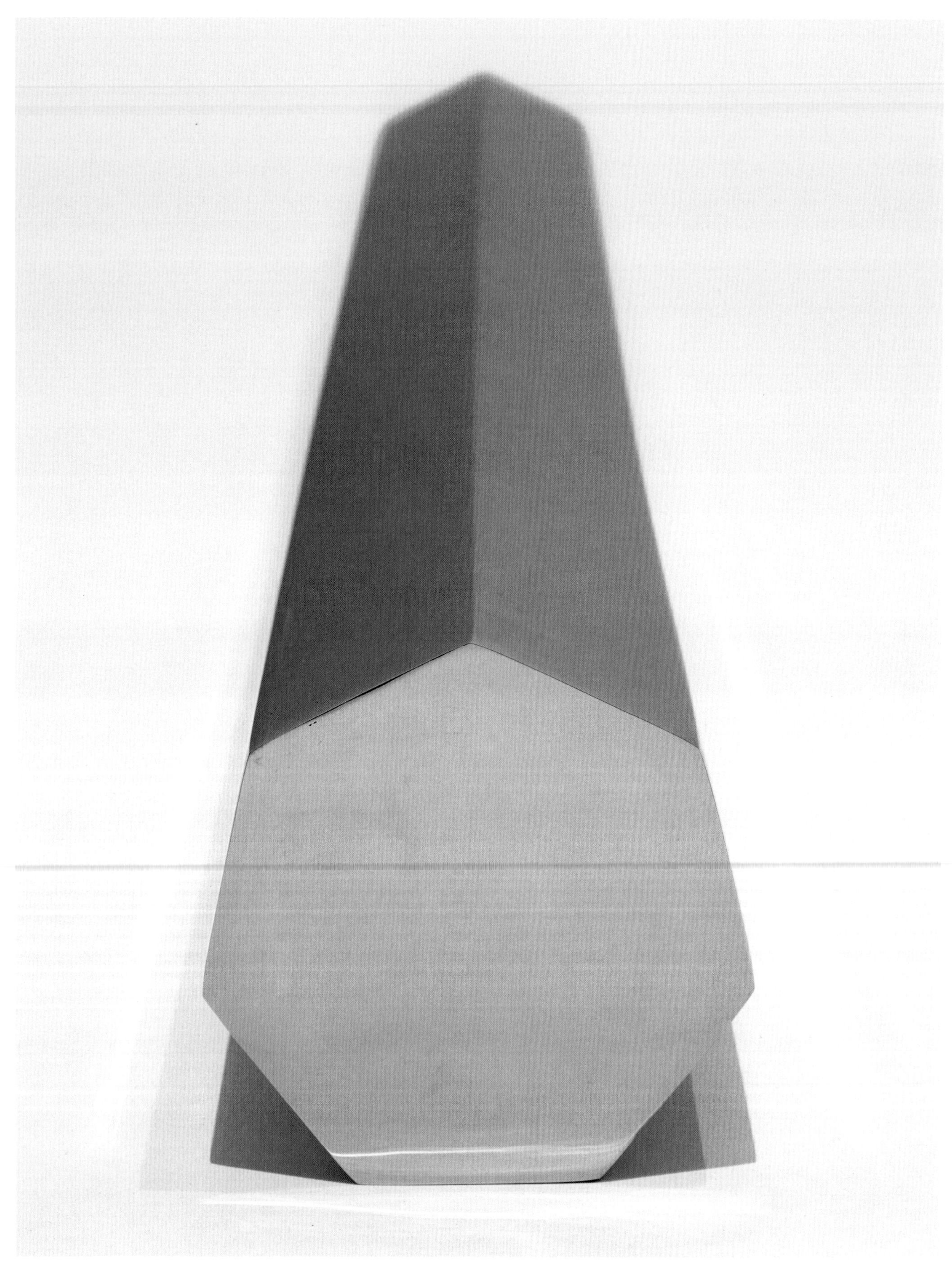

Fig. 22. Detail, 7-sided rod

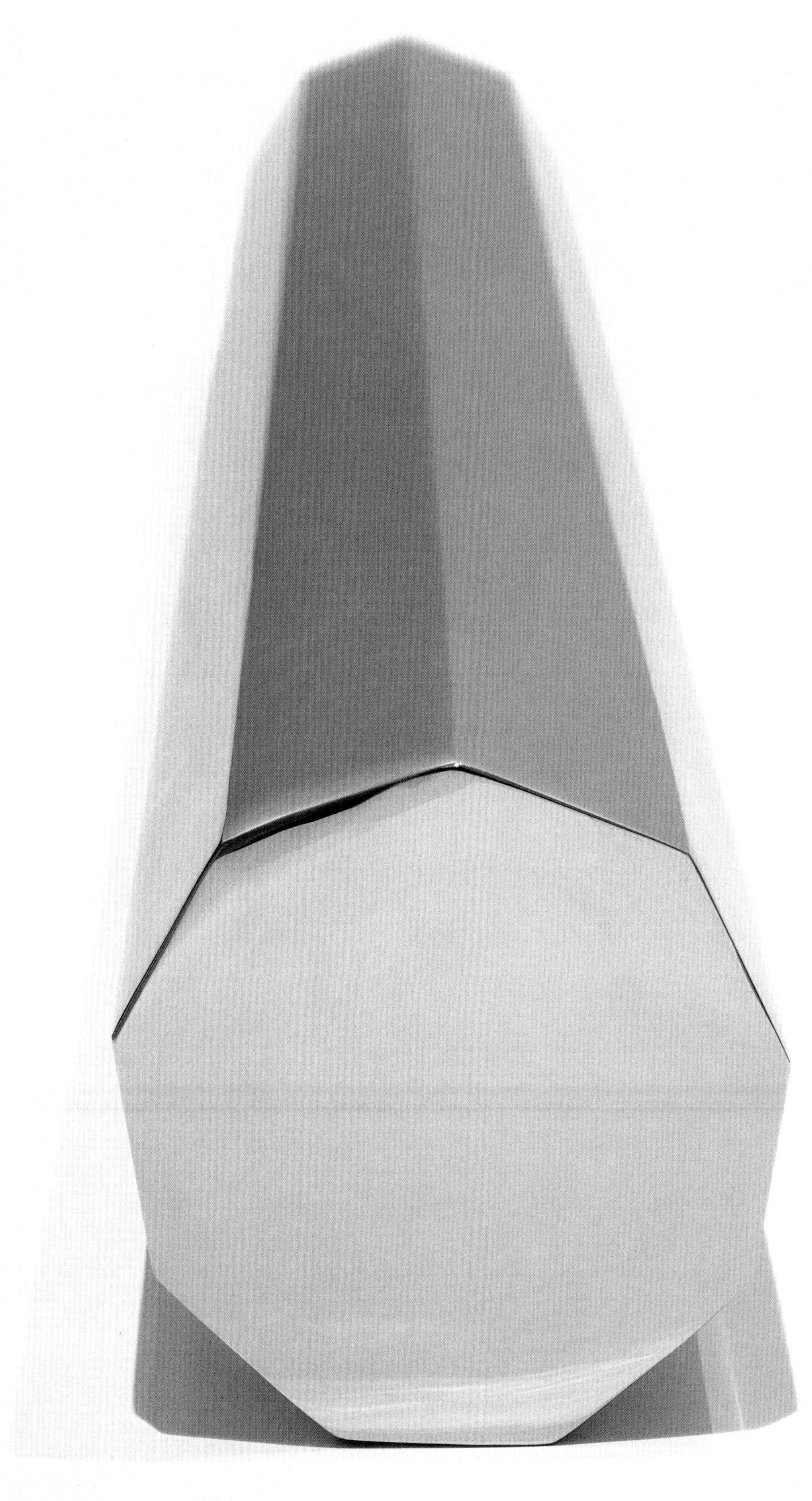

Fig. 23. Detail, 9-sided rod

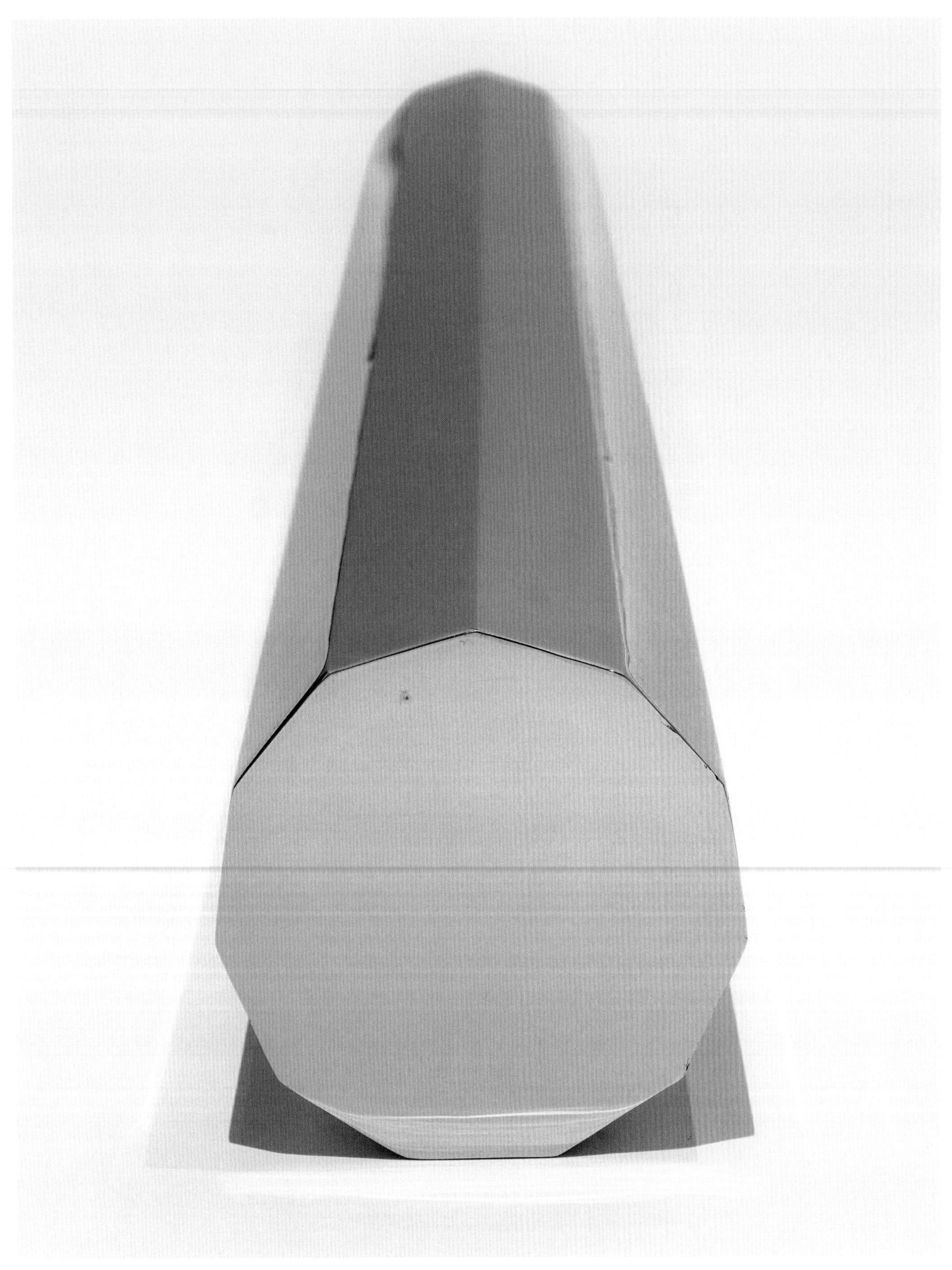

Fig. 24. Detail, 11-sided rod

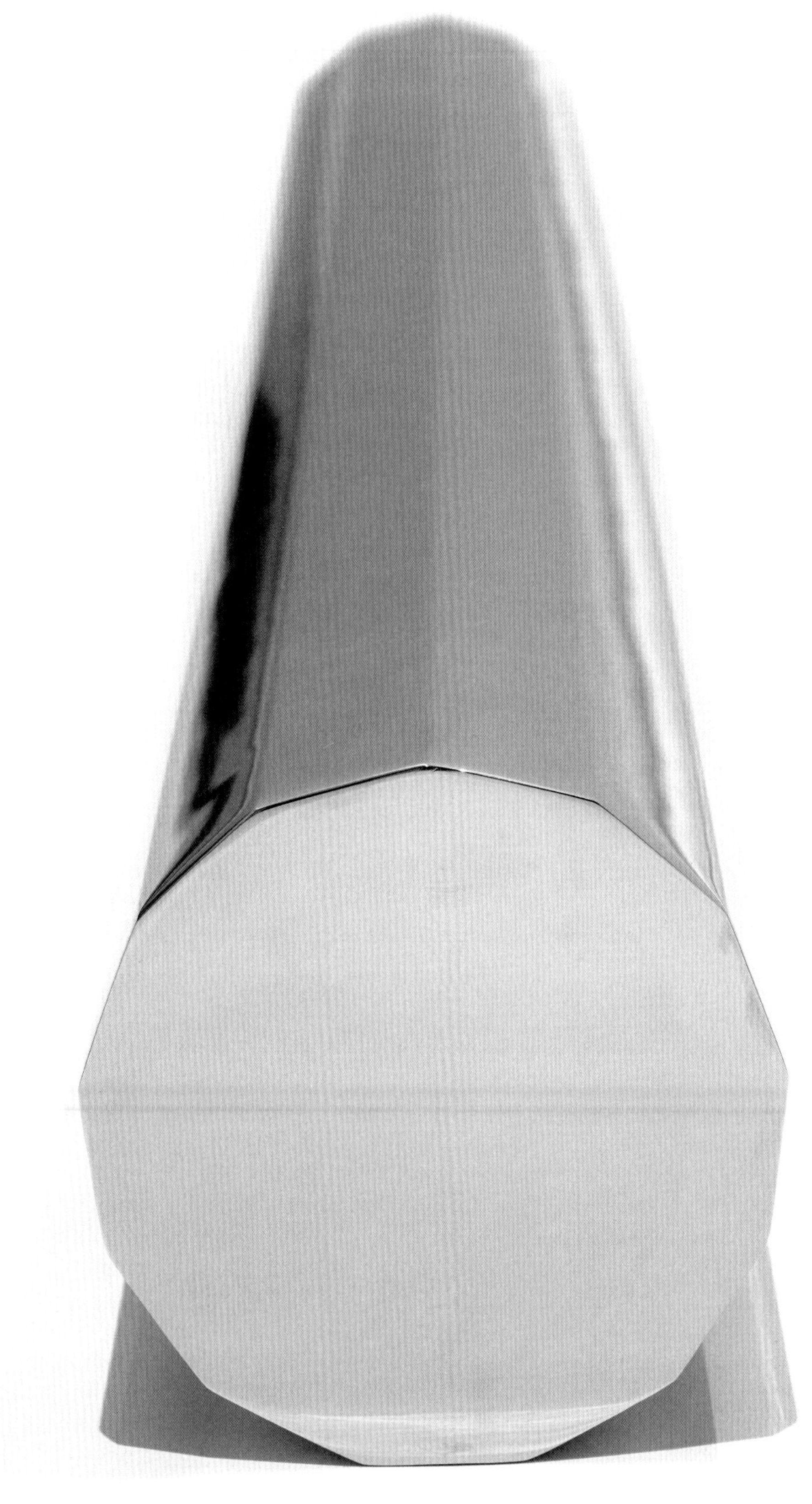

Fig. 25. Detail, 13-sided rod

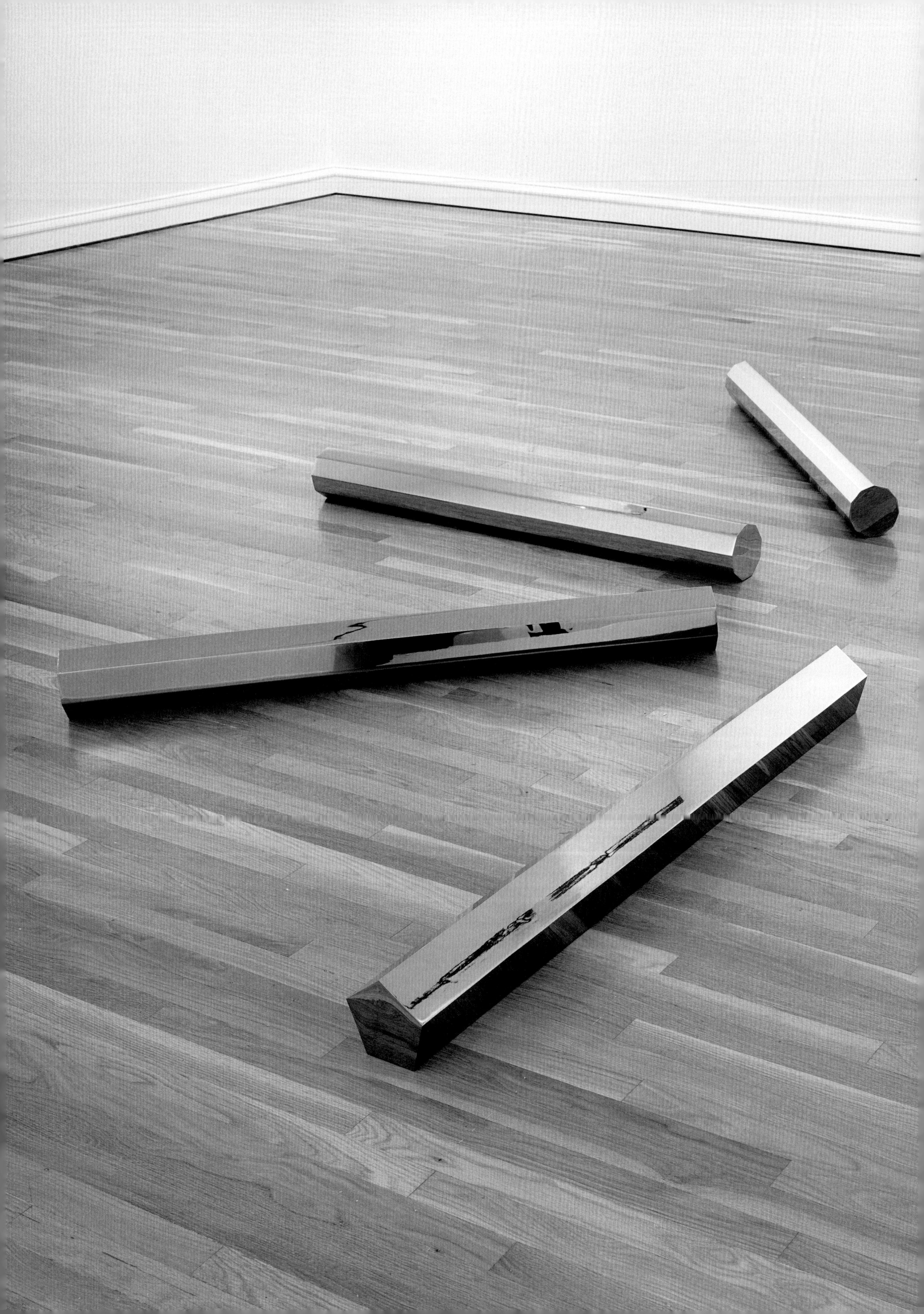

Fig. 26. Circle configuration with 8 rods. Diameter: 146½ in. (372 cm), using one 5-sided rod, two 7-sided rods, two 9-sided rods, two 11-sided rods, and one 13-sided rod

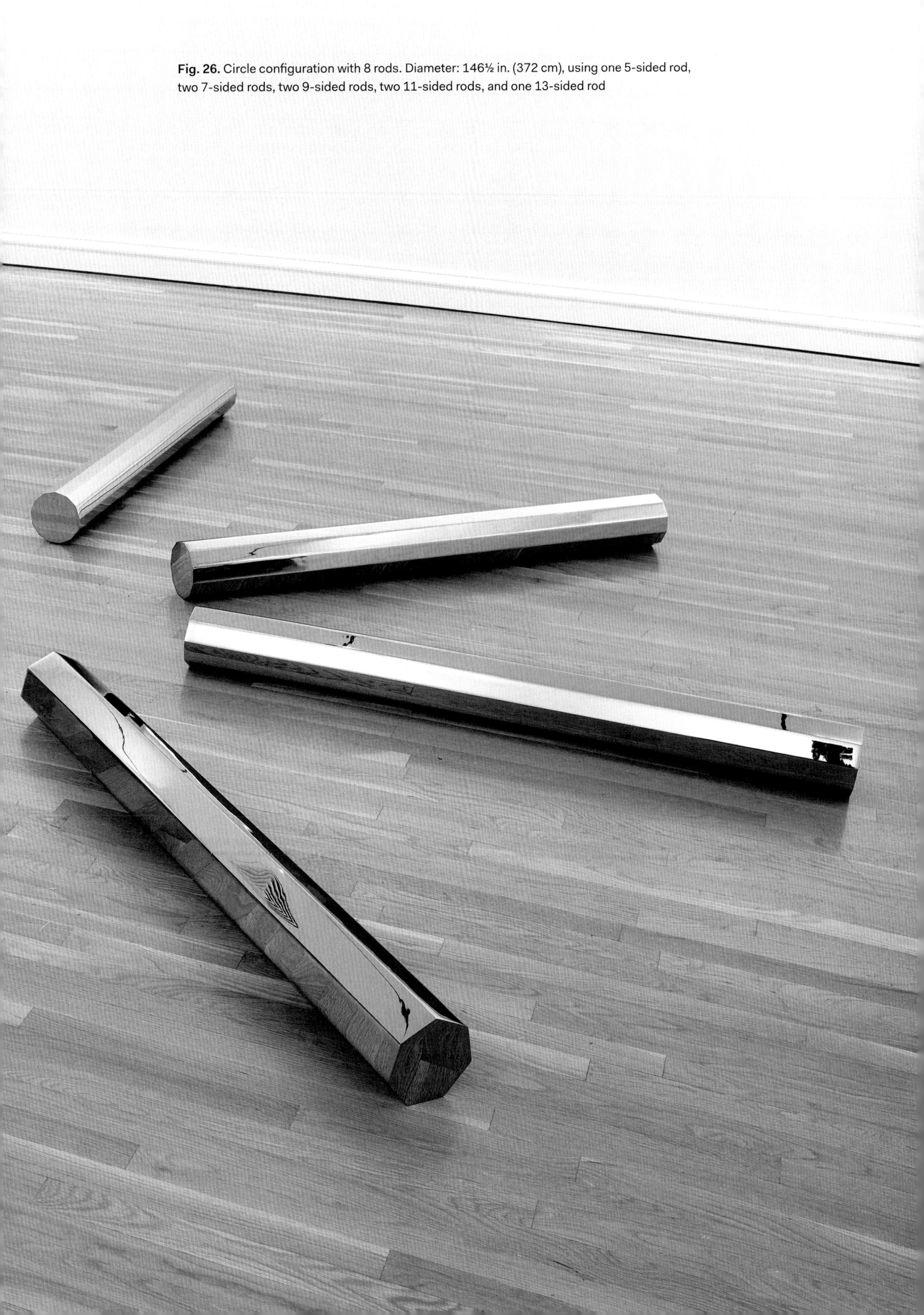

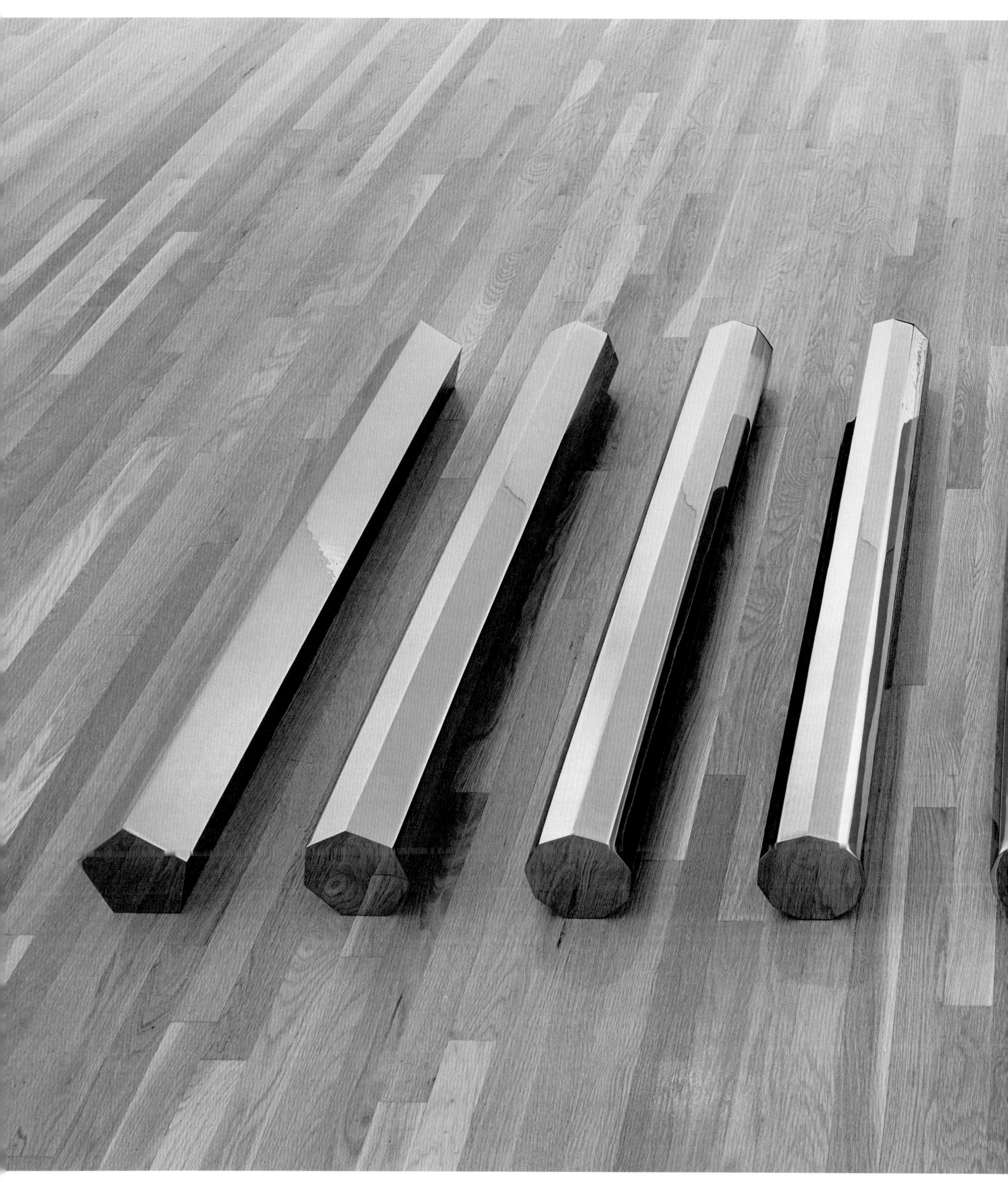

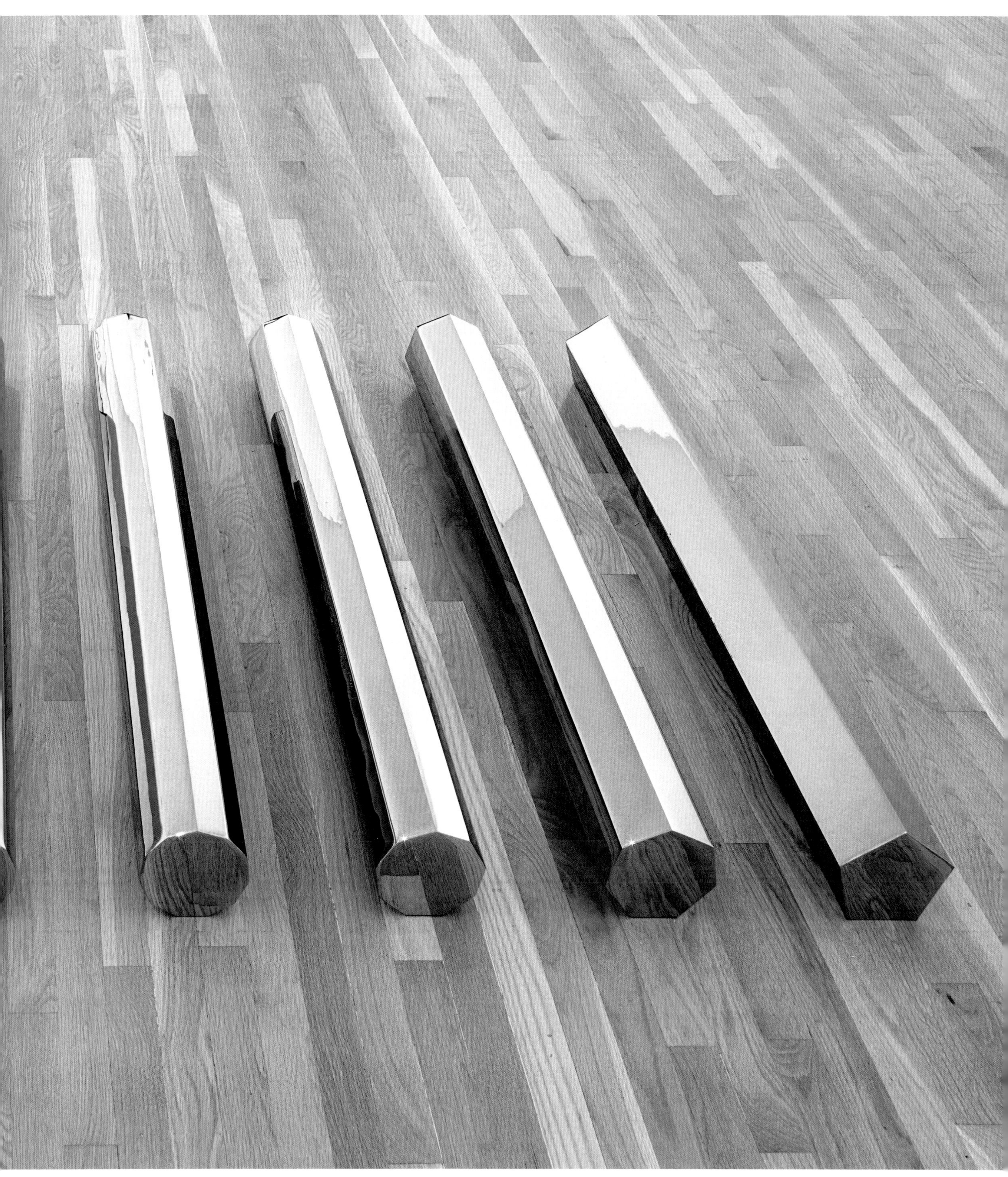

Fig. 27. Short rectangle configuration with 9 rods. Overall: 5⅜ x 52 x 94⅝ in.
(13.5 x 132 x 240 cm), using two 5-sided rods, two 7-sided rods, two 9-sided rods,
two 11-sided rods, and one 13-sided rod

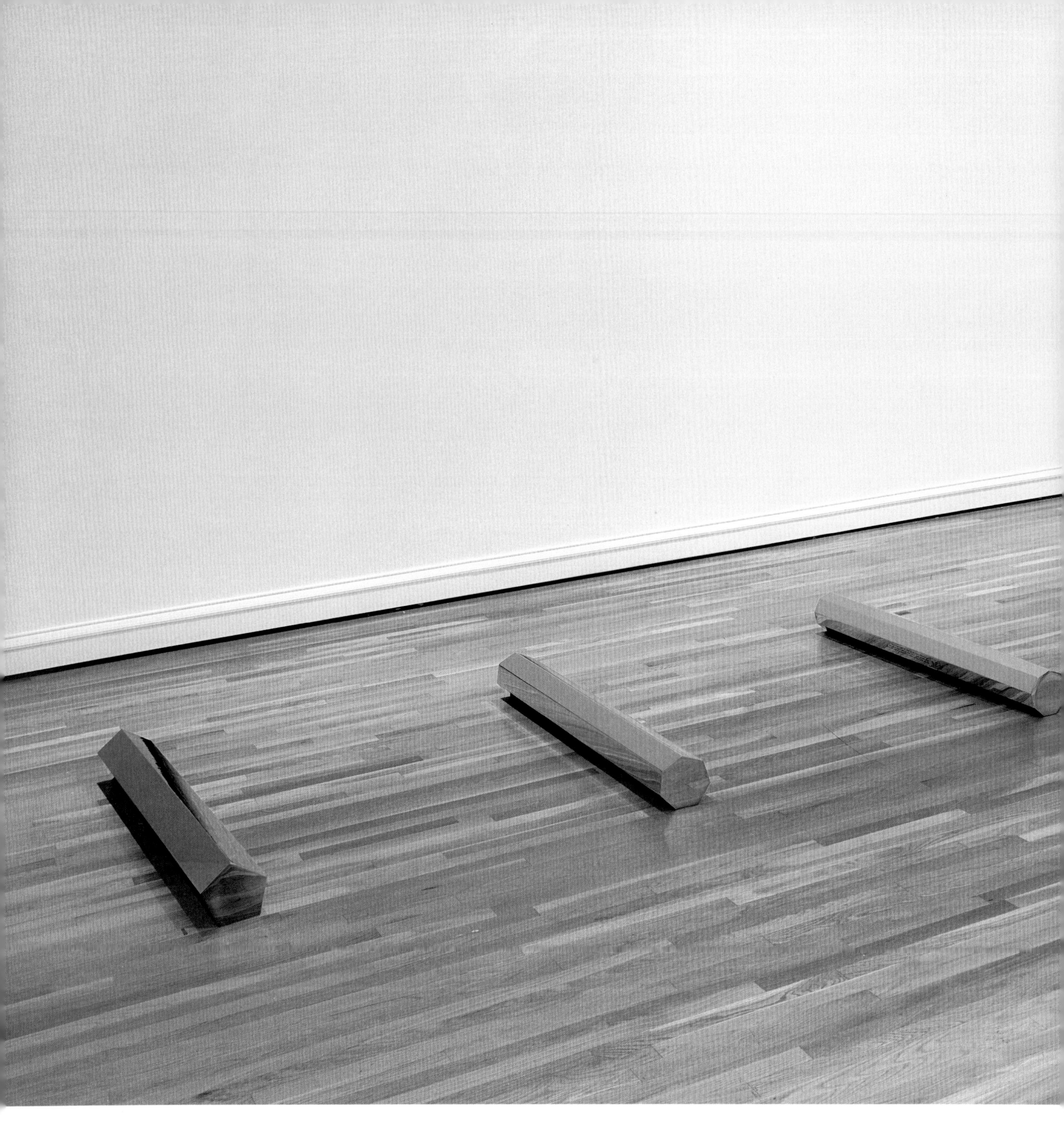

Fig. 28. Long rectangle configuration with 9 rods. Overall: 5⅜ x 52 x 362⅜ in.
(13.5 x 132 x 920.4 cm), using two 5-sided rods, two 7-sided rods, two 9-sided rods,
two 11-sided rods, and one 13-sided rod

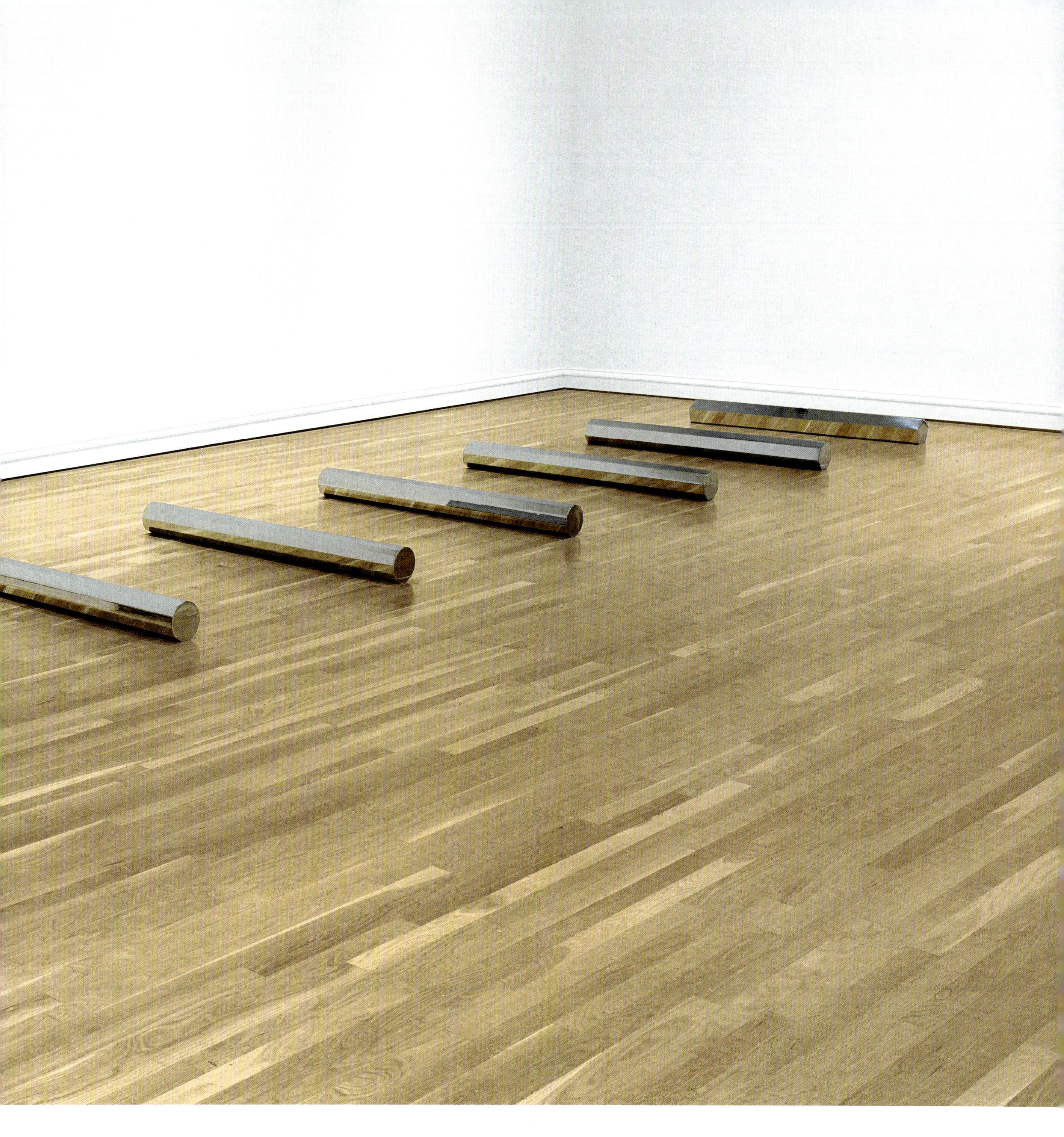

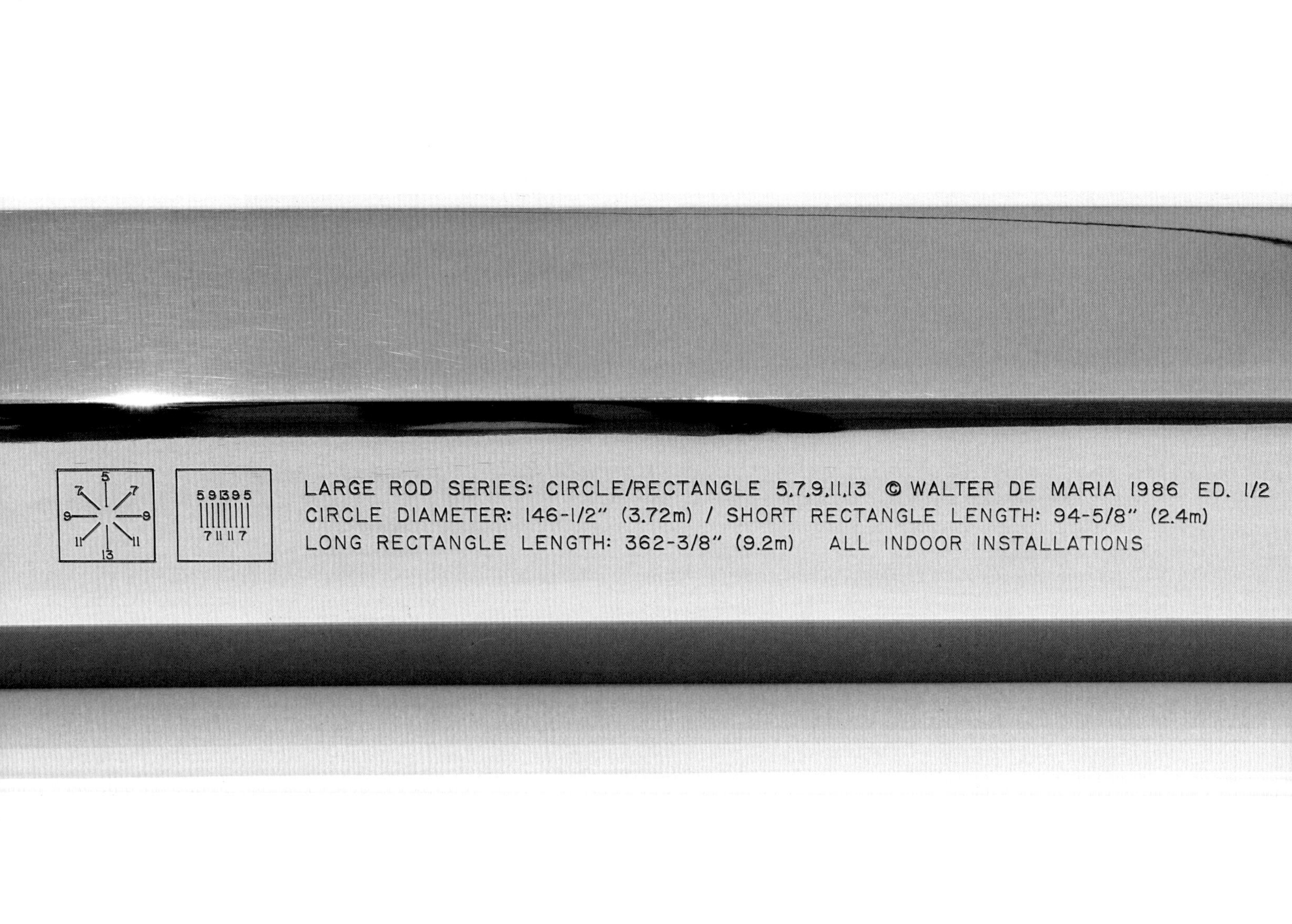

Fig. 29. Detail, artist's installation instructions engraved on the underside of each rod

Large Rod Series, 1984–1989

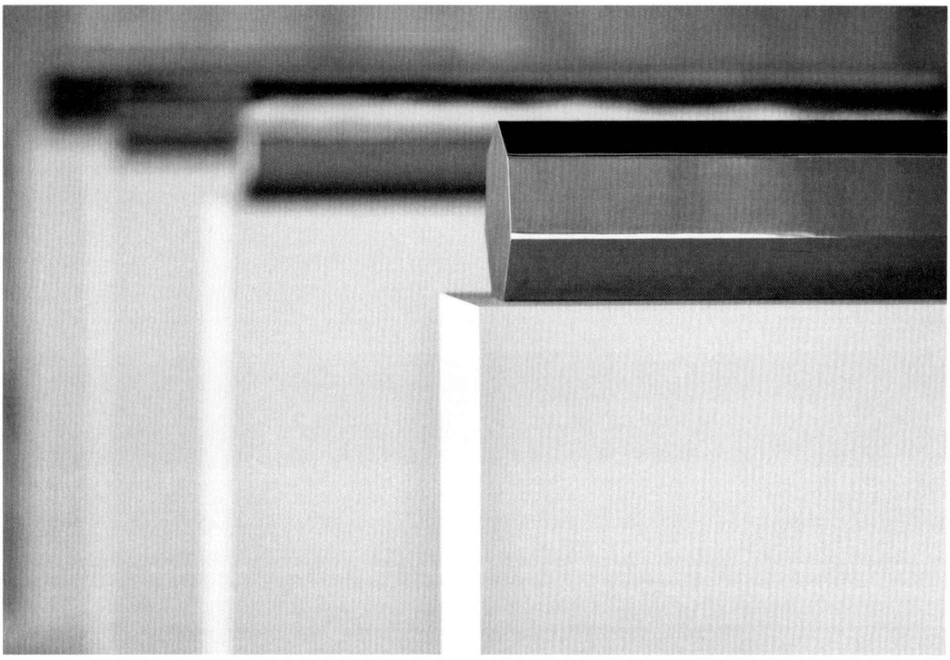

Fig. 30. Detail of *Large Rod Series: Pedestal Rods 5, 7, 9, 11, 13*, 1984

Fig. 31. *Large Rod Series: Pedestal Rods 5, 7, 9, 11, 13*, 1984. Stainless steel, overall 42⅞ x 54 x
352½ in. (108.7 x 137.2 x 895.2 cm), using one 5-sided rod, one 7-sided rod, one 9-sided rod,
one 11-sided rod, and one 13-sided rod, placed on wood pedestals. In background: *Pure Polygon
Series* (1975–1976). Private collection, NY

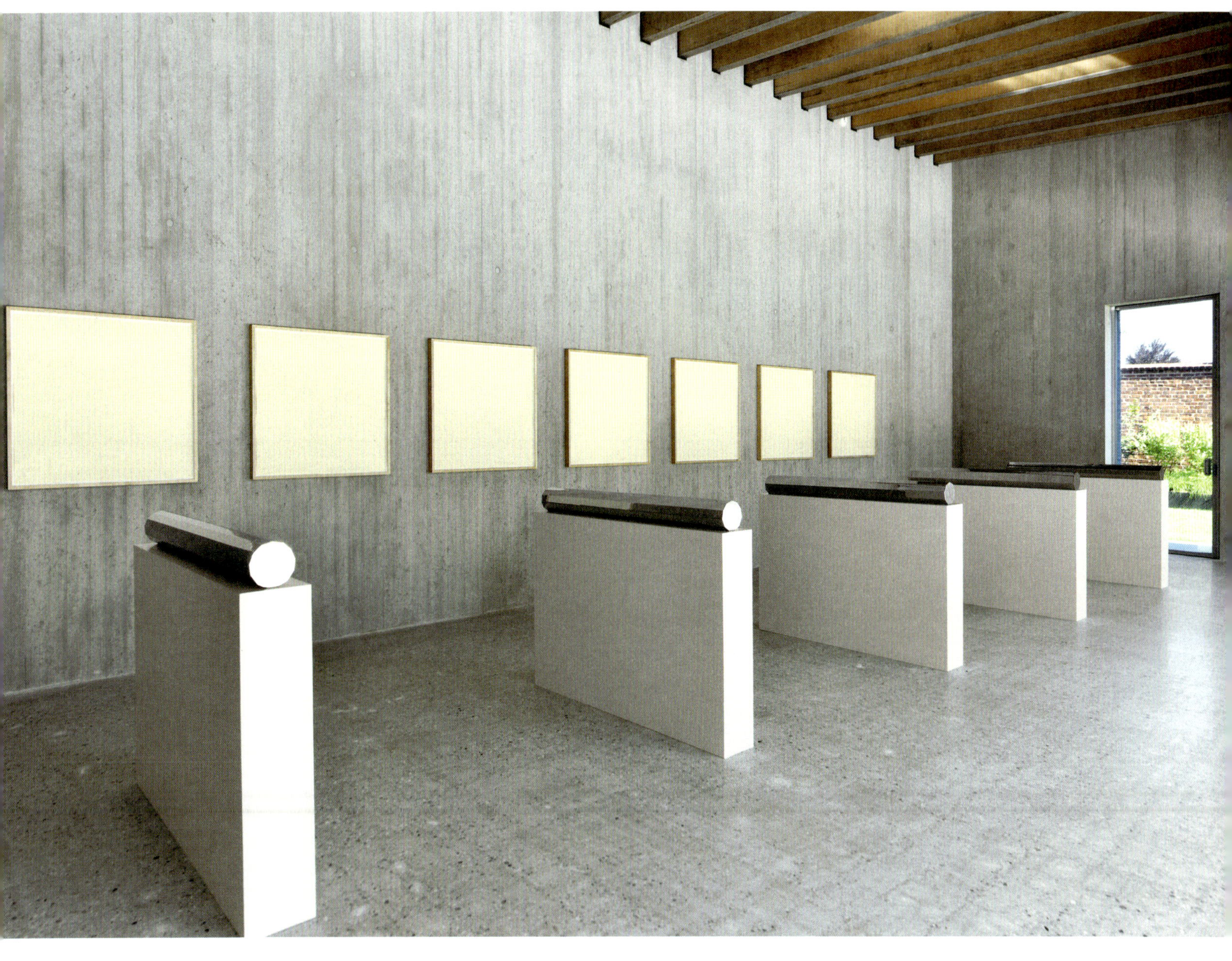

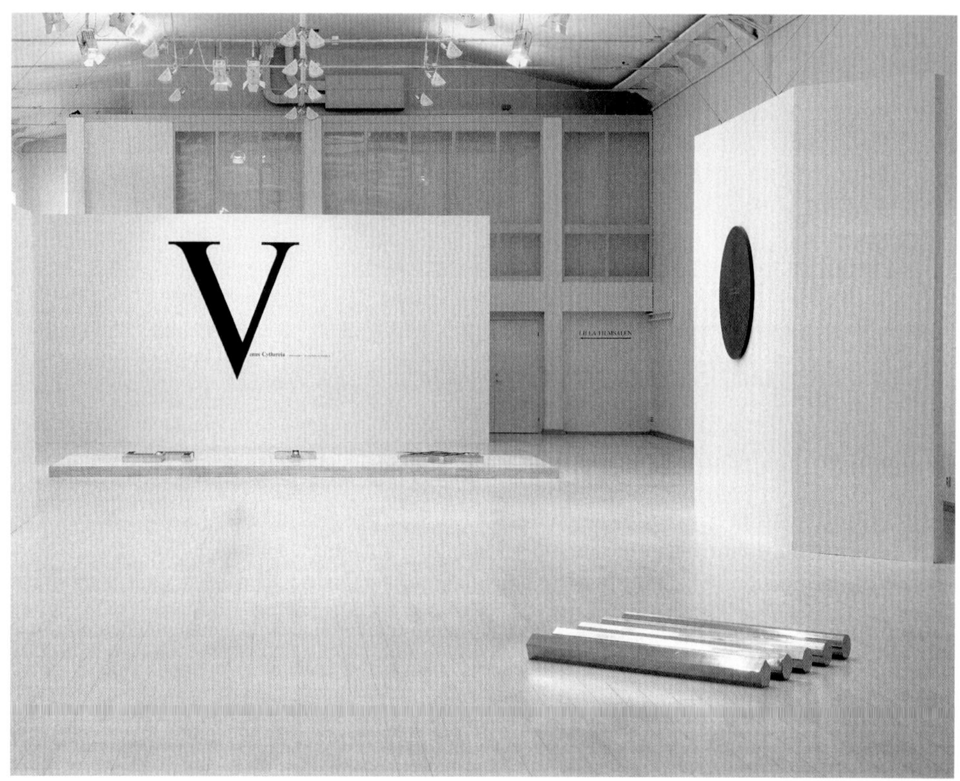

Fig. 32. Installation view of *Walter De Maria: Two Very Large Presentations*, Moderna Museet, Stockholm, March 11–May 7, 1989. In foreground: *Large Rod Series: Square 5, 7, 9, 11, 13*, 1984. Background, left to right: *Museum Piece* (1966), *Cross* (1965), *Star* (1972), and *There Exists in the Universe More Than One Billion Galaxies* (1988)

Fig. 33. *Large Rod Series: Square 5, 7, 9, 11, 13*, 1984. Stainless steel, overall 5⅜ x 51¾ x 51¾ in. (13.5 x 131.4 x 131.4 cm), using one 5-sided rod, one 7-sided rod, one 9-sided rod, one 11-sided rod, and one 13-sided rod. Moderna Museet, Stockholm

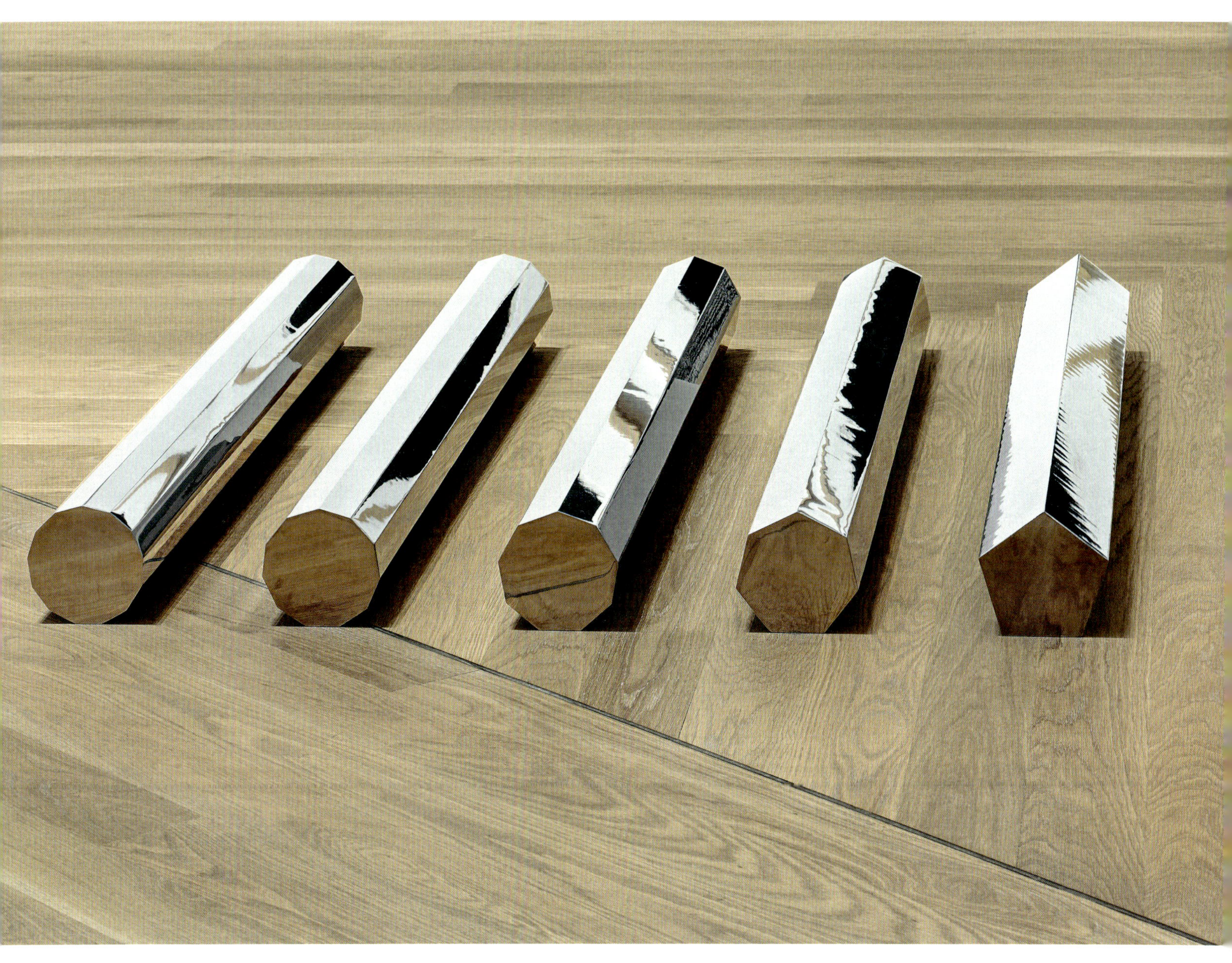

Fig. 34. *Large Rod Series: Circle/Rectangle 5, 7, 9, 11, 13*, 1985. Edition 2/2. Stainless steel, short rectangle overall: 5⅜ x 51¾ x 94⅝ in. (13.5 x 131.4 x 240 cm), using two 5-sided rods, two 7-sided rods, two 9-sided rods, two 11-sided rods, and one 13-sided rod. Rolla Collection, Switzerland

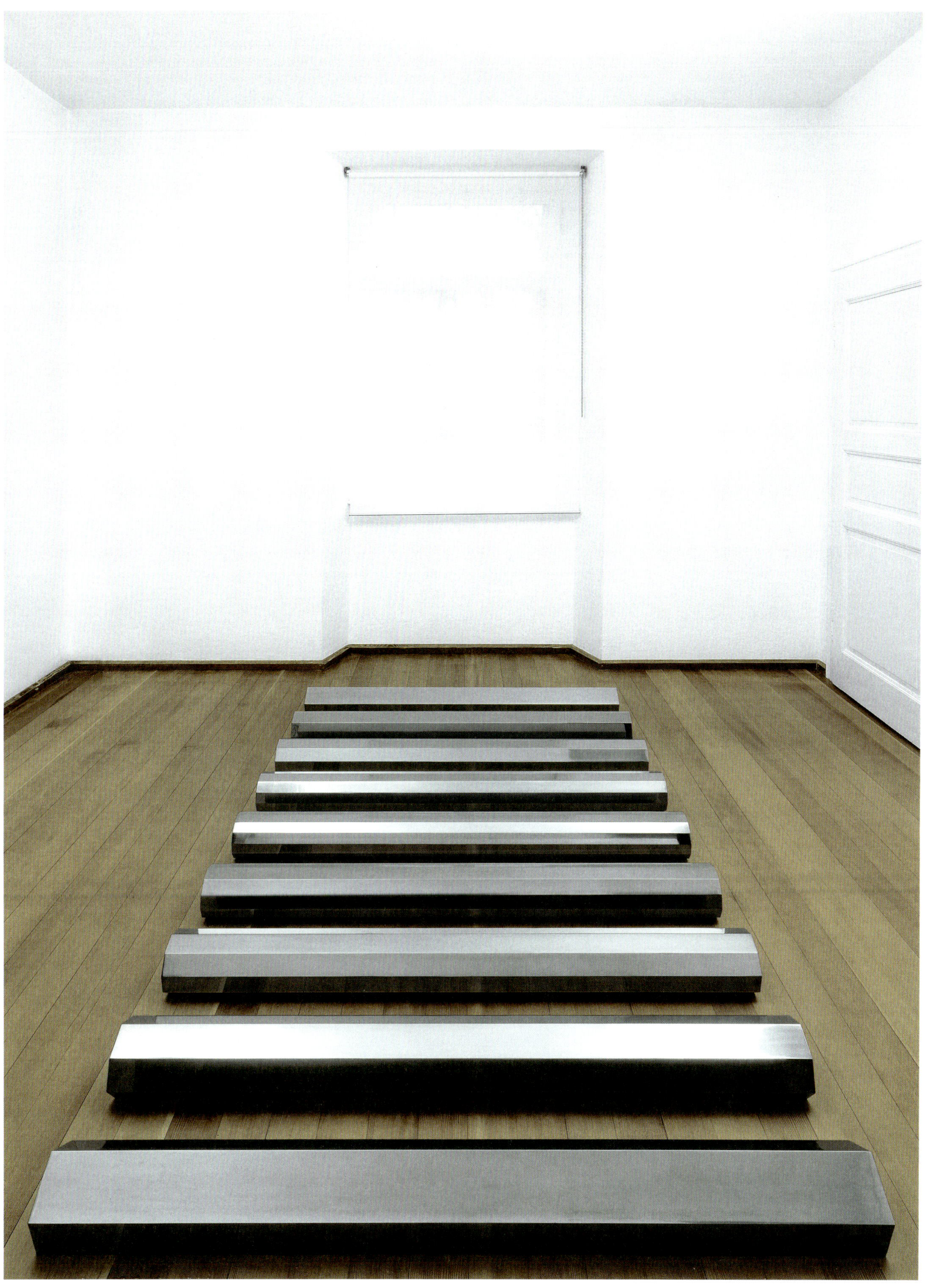

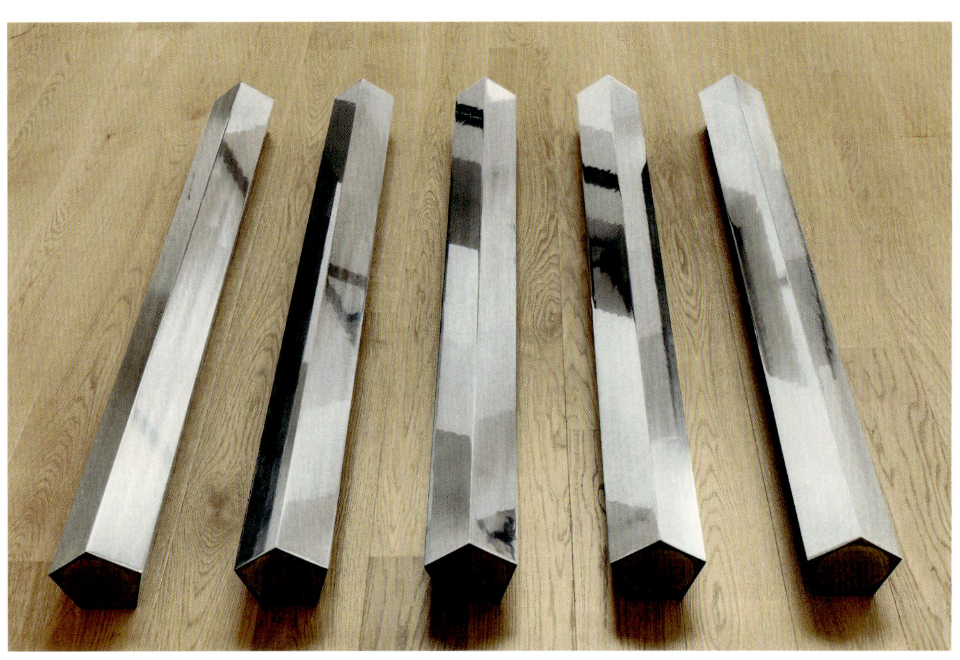

Figs. 35–36. *Large Rod Series: Circle/Rectangle 5*, 1986. Stainless steel, short rectangle overall: 5⅜ x 52 x 50⅛ in. (13.5 x 132 x 127 cm), using five 5-sided rods. Private collection

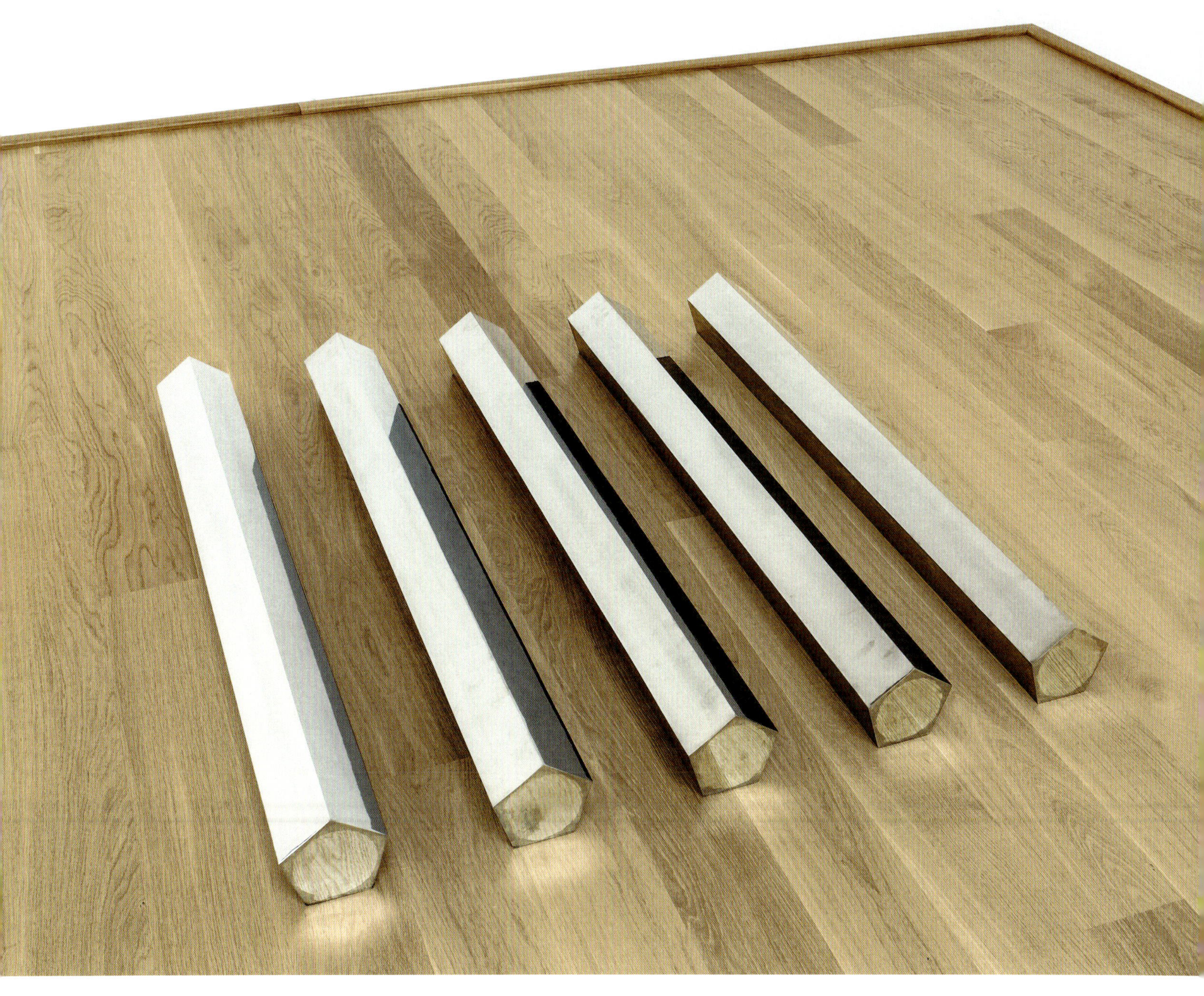

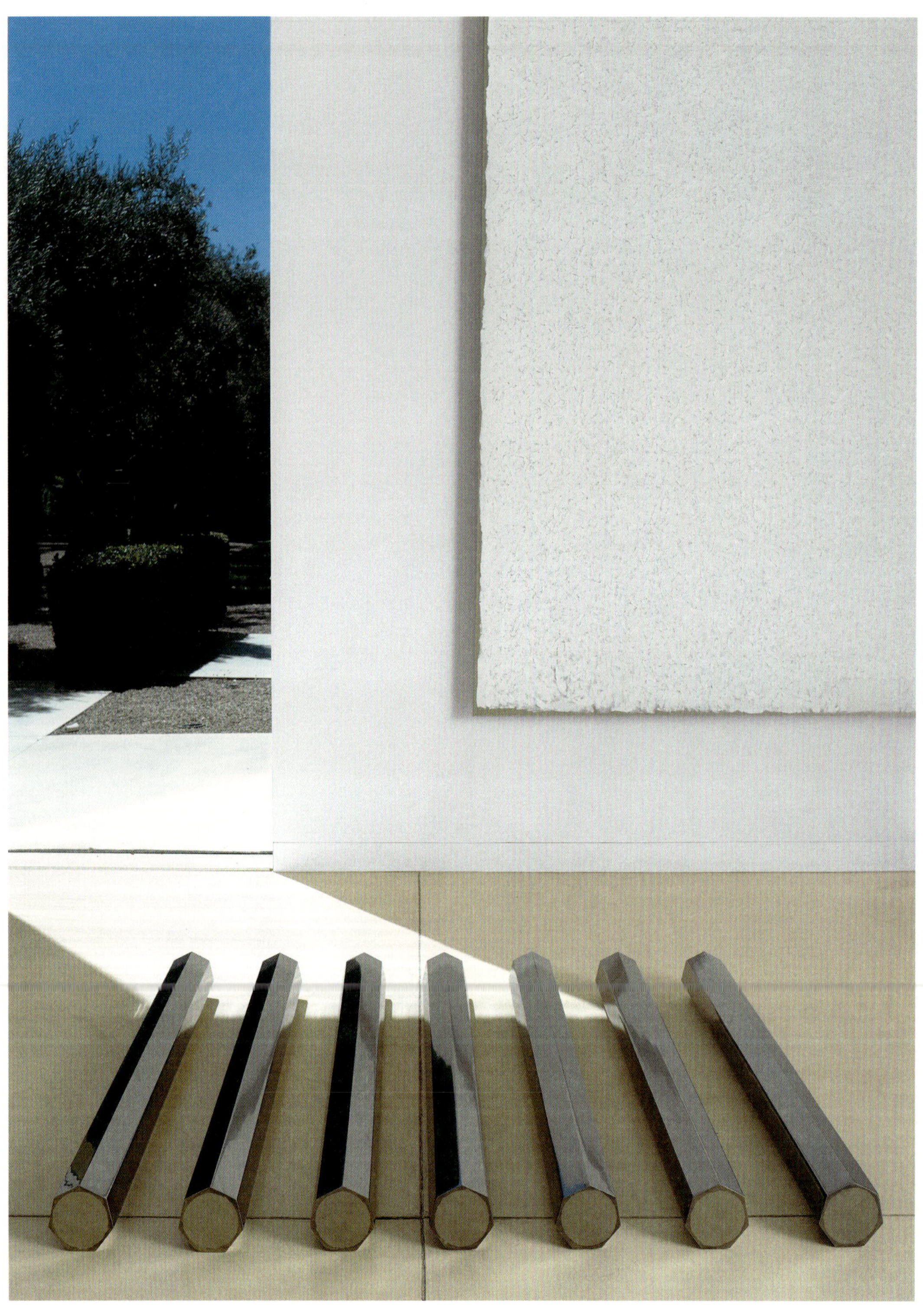

Figs. 37–38. *Large Rod Series: Circle/Rectangle 7*, 1986. Stainless steel, short rectangle overall: 5⅜ x 52 x 69⅝ in. (13.5 x 132 x 176 cm), using seven 7-sided rods. Collection Frances and John Bowes

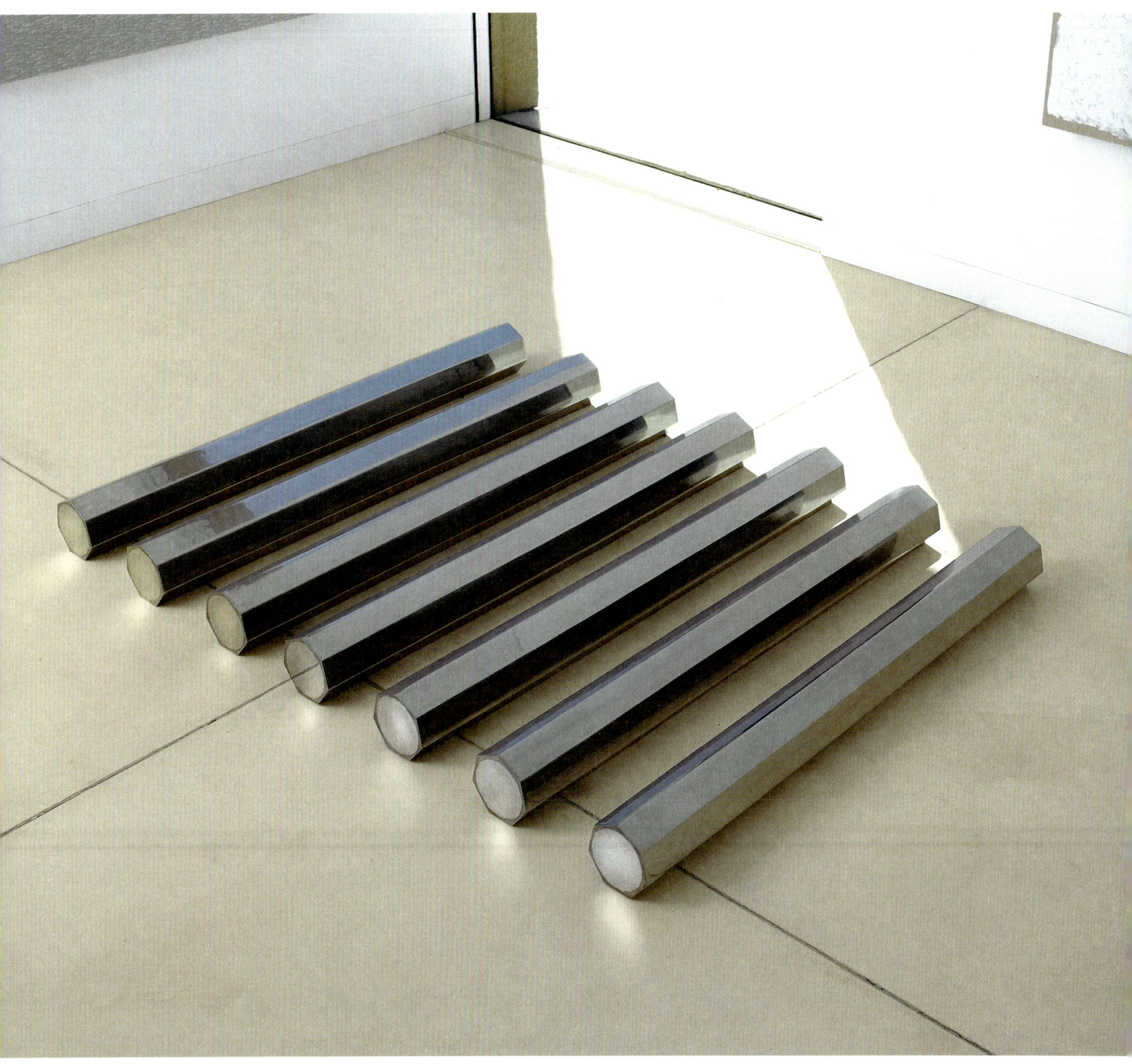

Fig. 39. *Large Rod Series: Circle/Rectangle 9*, 1986. Stainless steel, circle configuration.
Diameter: 149⅝ in. (379 cm), using nine 9-sided rods. Private collection

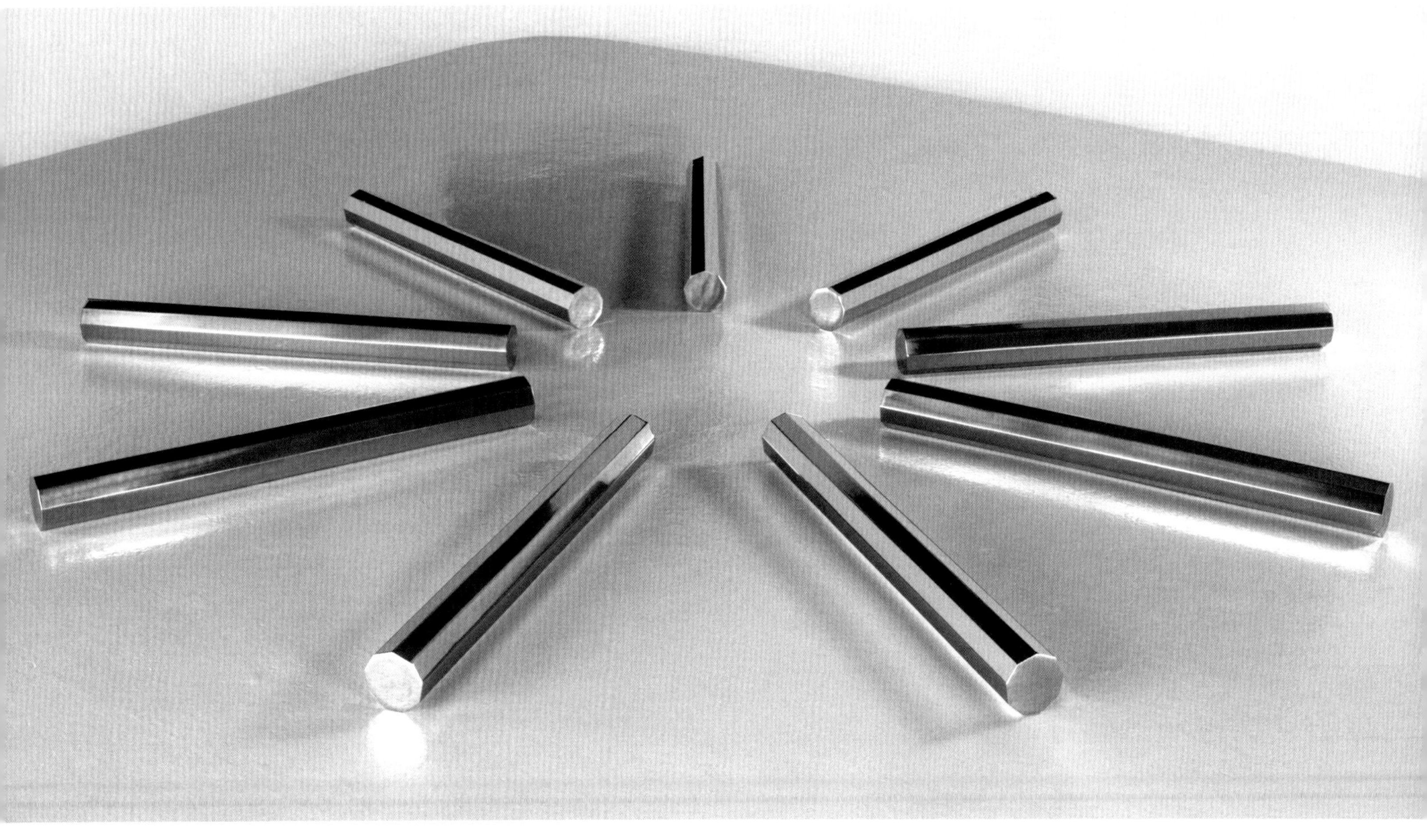

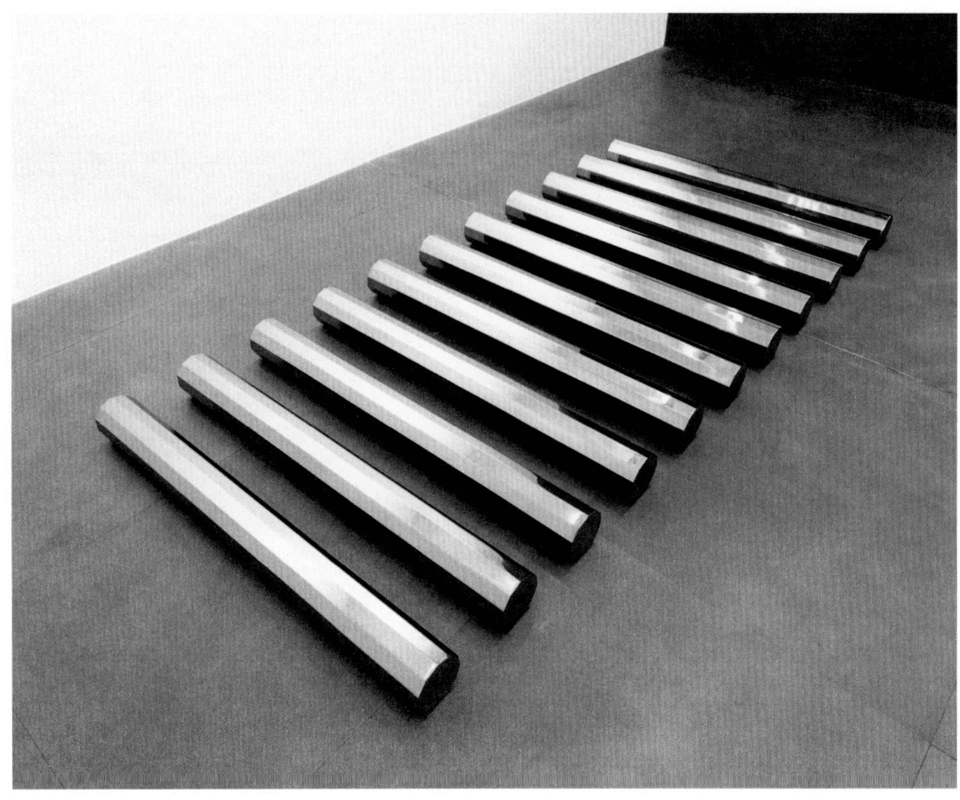

Figs. 40–41. *Large Rod Series: Circle/Rectangle 11*, 1986. Stainless steel, short rectangle overall: 5⅟₁₆ x 52 x 109⅜ in. (13 x 132 x 277 cm), using eleven 11-sided rods. Private collection. Courtesy Gagosian Gallery

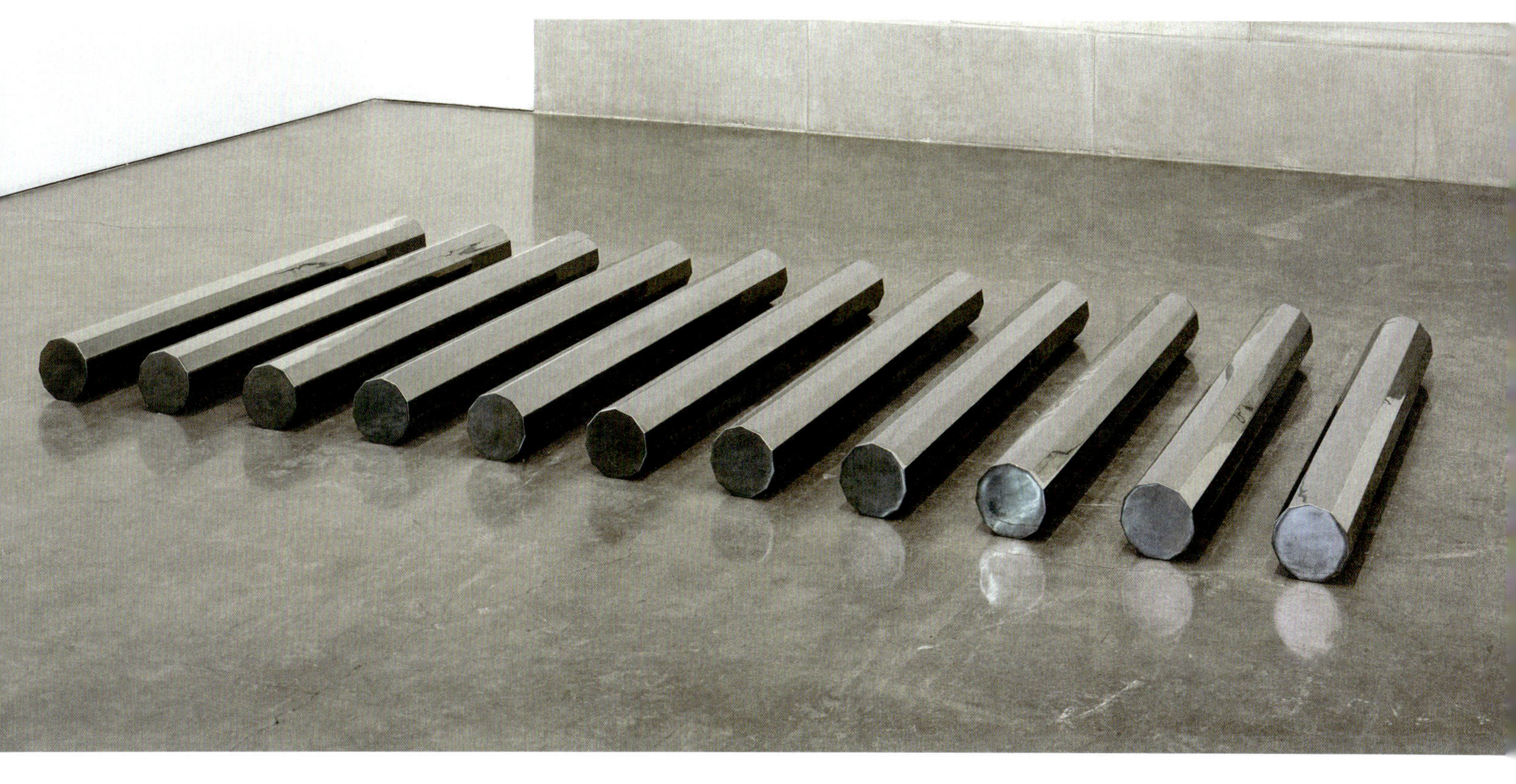

Fig 42. *Large Rod Series: Circle/Rectangle 13*, 1986. Stainless steel, long rectangle overall: 5⅜ x 52 x 362⅜ in. (13.5 x 132 x 920.43 cm), using thirteen 13-sided rods. Magasin III Museum & Foundation for Contemporary Art, Stockholm, Sweden

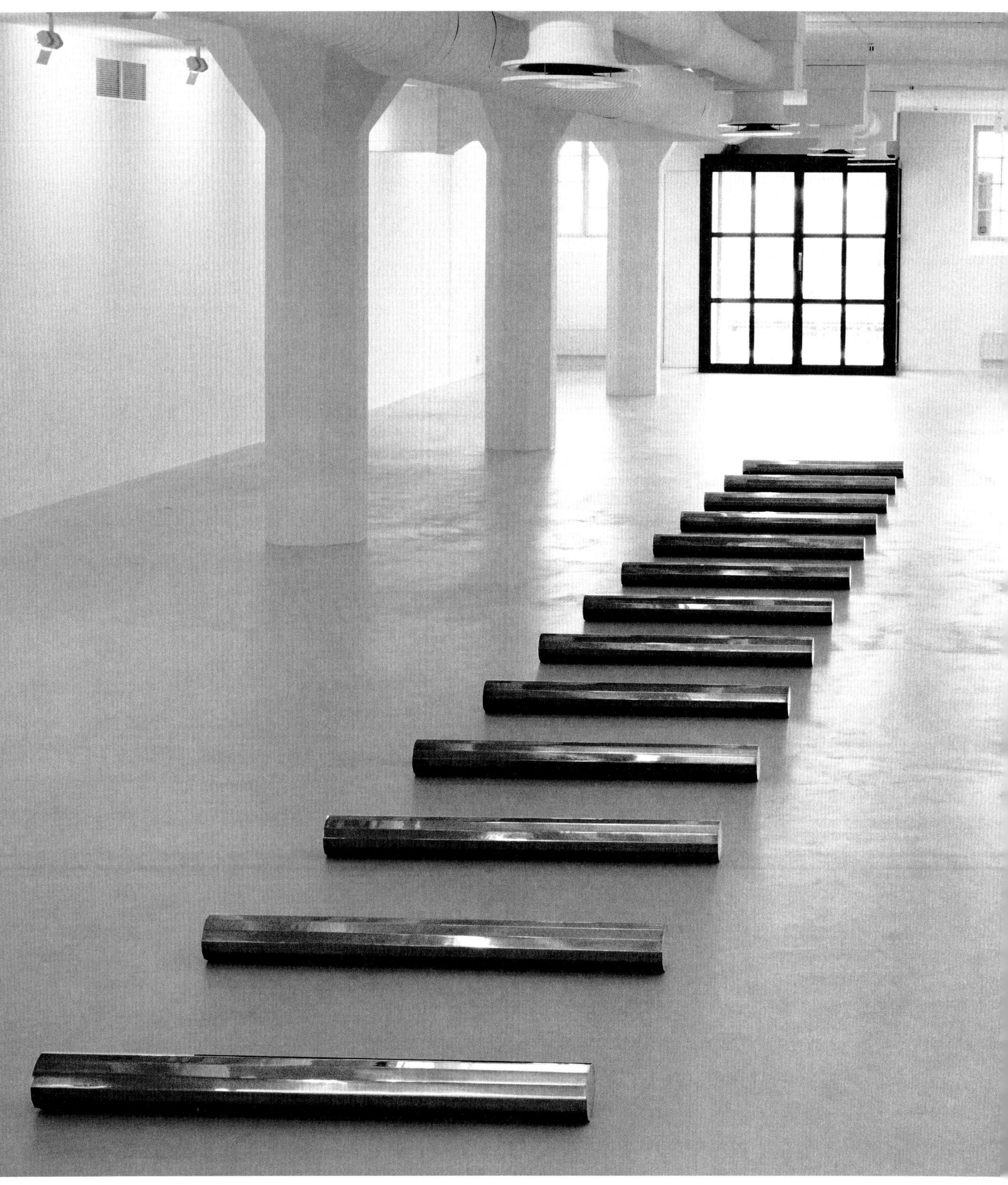

Fig 43. *Large Rod Series: Rectangle 7/11*, 1989. Stainless steel, short rectangle overall: 5¹⁄₁₆ x
52 x 91 in. (13 x 132 x 231 cm), using five 7-sided rods and four 11-sided rods. Kouri Collection,
Museum of Contemporary Art Kiasma, Helsinki

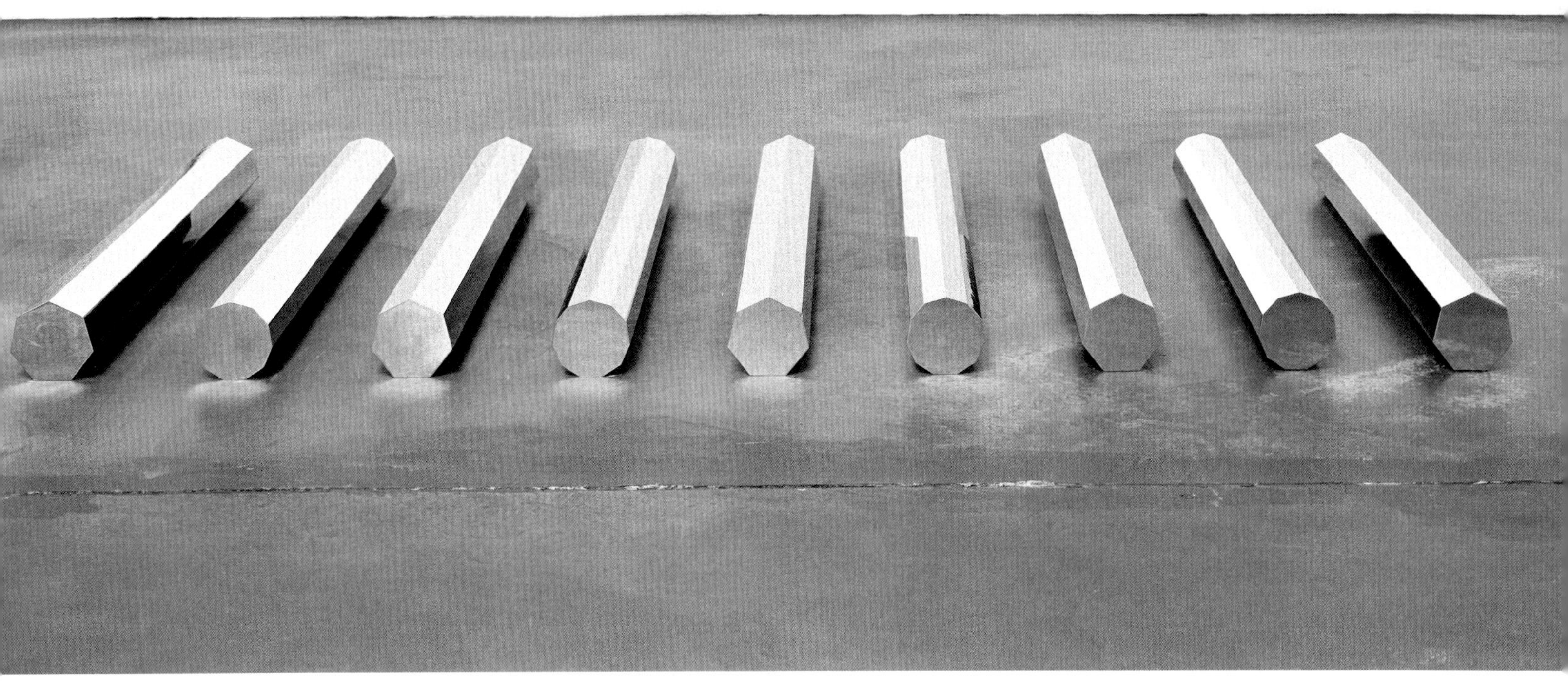

Large Rod Series Installation Notes
by Walter De Maria

Notes

The *Large Rod Series* presently consists of eight sculptures produced between 1984 and 1986. Each sculpture is comprised of a specific number of custom-made stainless steel polygonal bars. Each bar is 5, 7, 9, 11 or 13-sided. These elements are arranged in either a *Square, Circle, Short Rectangle* or *Long Rectangle* of definite dimension.

Two types of stainless steel bars were fabricated for the series. The first type is solid, weighs 300 pounds and is used in the *Pedestal Rods 5, 7, 9, 11, 13, Square 5, 7, 9, 11, 13* and *Circle/Rectangle 5, 7, 9, 11, 13* edition 1/2. These bars were custom-milled, hand ground and hand polished. The second type of bar weighs between 119 and 142 pounds, depending on the number of facets on the bar and is used in the *Circle/Rectangle 5, 7, 9, 11, 13* edition 2/2, and *Circle/Rectangle 5* through *Circle/Rectangle 13*. These bars were drawn through custom-made dies, hand welded, machine ground, hand ground and hand polished. The length of the first type of bars is 51¾″ (131.4 cm.) and the length of the second type of bars is 52″ (132 cm.).

Bar dimensions:

	height	*width*
5-sided	5⁵⁄₁₆″ (13.5 cm.)	5¹⁰⁄₁₆″ (14.4 cm.)
7-sided	5⁵⁄₁₆″ (13.4 cm.)	5⁶⁄₁₆″ (13.8 cm.)
9-sided	5³⁄₁₆″ (13.2 cm.)	5⁵⁄₁₆″ (13.4 cm.)
11-sided	5¹⁄₁₆″ (13 cm.)	5³⁄₁₆″ (13.2 cm.)
13-sided	5³⁄₁₆″ (13.2 cm.)	5³⁄₁₆″ (13.2 cm.)

The first piece in the series, *Pedestal Rods 5, 7, 9, 11, 13,* displayed each polygonal bar in sequence on narrow pedestals measuring 37½″ (95 cm.) high placed 2 meters apart (see photo page 26).

The second piece in the series, *Square 5, 7, 9, 11, 13,* again presented five parallel rods in the same sequence, this time arranged directly on the floor to form a *Square* (see cover photo). This sculpture was exhibited in the premier exhibition of the Museum of Art, Fort Lauderdale, "American Renaissance: Painting and Sculpture Since 1940," in Spring 1986.

The third sculpture of the series, *Circle/Rectangle 5, 7, 9, 11, 13,* increased the number of bars beyond the original five. Nine bars were used to create the *Rectangle* and eight bars were used to make the *Circle.* In both the *Rectangle* and the *Circle* ascending and descending numerical patterns were used to form a continuum. The qualities and possibilities of the *Circle* changing to a *Rectangle* and the *Rectangle* changing to the *Circle* evolved during the creation of this work. It was at a later time in the development of the *Large Rod Series* that the possibility of expanding the *Short Rectangles* to the *Long Rectangles* became apparent. This option now exists in the *Circle/Rectangle* sculptures of the series. These works, therefore, possess three formal installation configuration possibilities: *Circle, Short Rectangle* or *Long Rectangle.* These transformations are completely optional. A work may remain forever in one form should this be decided.

The *Rectangle* was exhibited in the "New Works" exhibition series at the Sackler Wing of the Fogg Museum, Harvard University, Boston in February 1986 (see photo page 5). The *Circle* configuration of *Circle/Rectangle 5, 7, 9, 11, 13* will be presented for the first time in this exhibition (see photo page 3).

The next five pieces in the *Large Rod Series* are: *Circle/Rectangle 5* [five 5-sided rods], *Circle/Rectangle 7* [seven 7-sided rods], *Circle/Rectangle 9* [nine 9-sided rods], *Circle/Rectangle 11* [eleven 11-sided rods] and *Circle/Rectangle 13* [thirteen 13-sided rods]. In these sculptures the shape of a single bar creates the "theme" and number of rods in the sculpture. The option of three installation configurations also exists in these five works. These sculptures are unique, edition 1/1.

> Installation placement and spacing:
>
> *Circles:* a two bar-width space module is used for placing the bars in the interior circle space. All bars radiate from the center equally.
>
> *Short Rectangles:* a one bar-width space is the module used between each parallel bar.
>
> *Long Rectangles:* One meter is the space used between each parallel bar.

Engraved inscriptions on floor-side facet of each bar in the Circle/Rectangle sculptures

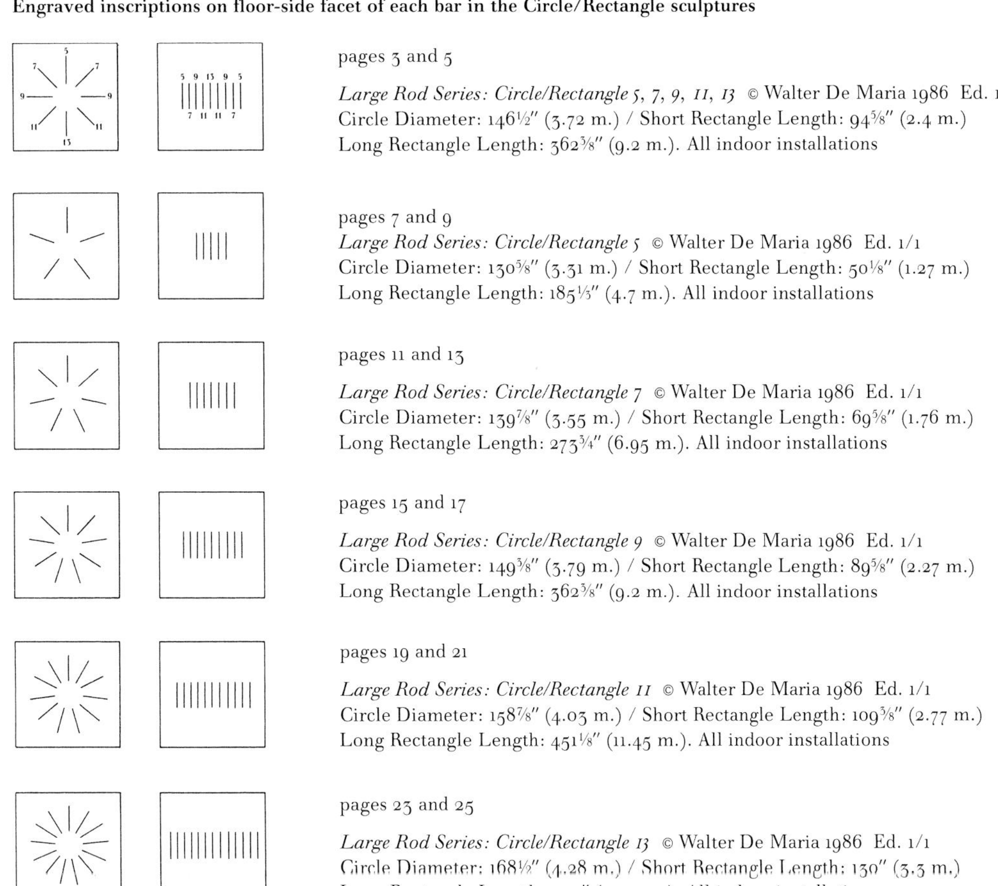

pages 3 and 5

Large Rod Series: Circle/Rectangle 5, 7, 9, 11, 13 © Walter De Maria 1986 Ed. 1/2
Circle Diameter: 146½″ (3.72 m.) / Short Rectangle Length: 94⅝″ (2.4 m.)
Long Rectangle Length: 362⅜″ (9.2 m.). All indoor installations

pages 7 and 9
Large Rod Series: Circle/Rectangle 5 © Walter De Maria 1986 Ed. 1/1
Circle Diameter: 130⅜″ (3.31 m.) / Short Rectangle Length: 50⅛″ (1.27 m.)
Long Rectangle Length: 185⅓″ (4.7 m.). All indoor installations

pages 11 and 13

Large Rod Series: Circle/Rectangle 7 © Walter De Maria 1986 Ed. 1/1
Circle Diameter: 139⅞″ (3.55 m.) / Short Rectangle Length: 69⅝″ (1.76 m.)
Long Rectangle Length: 273¾″ (6.95 m.). All indoor installations

pages 15 and 17

Large Rod Series: Circle/Rectangle 9 © Walter De Maria 1986 Ed. 1/1
Circle Diameter: 149⅜″ (3.79 m.) / Short Rectangle Length: 89⅝″ (2.27 m.)
Long Rectangle Length: 362⅜″ (9.2 m.). All indoor installations

pages 19 and 21

Large Rod Series: Circle/Rectangle 11 © Walter De Maria 1986 Ed. 1/1
Circle Diameter: 158⅞″ (4.03 m.) / Short Rectangle Length: 109⅜″ (2.77 m.)
Long Rectangle Length: 451⅛″ (11.45 m.). All indoor installations

pages 23 and 25

Large Rod Series: Circle/Rectangle 13 © Walter De Maria 1986 Ed. 1/1
Circle Diameter: 168½″ (4.28 m.) / Short Rectangle Length: 130″ (3.3 m.)
Long Rectangle Length: 540″ (13.71 m.). All indoor installations

Reproduced from *Walter De Maria: Large Rod Series, Circles/Rectangles, 1984–1986*, pp. 27–28.
Exh. cat. New York: Xavier Fourcade Gallery, 1986.

Walter De Maria: A Short Biography

Walter De Maria was born in 1935 in Albany, California, and died in 2013 in Los Angeles. From 1953 to 1959 he studied at the University of California, Berkeley, where he received his BA in history and his MA in art. De Maria's work has been shown extensively around the world in numerous solo and group exhibitions.

Solo shows include Dia: Beacon, New York (2016); Los Angeles County Museum of Art (2012–2013); The Menil Collection, Houston (2011); Museum Brandhorst, Munich (2010); De Pont Foundation for Contemporary Art, Tilburg, The Netherlands (2005); Nelson-Atkins Museum of Art, Kansas City, Missouri (2002); Kunsthaus Zürich (1999), traveled to Nationalgalerie im Hamburger Bahnhof, Hamburg, and Staatliche Museen zu Berlin (2000); Fondazione Prada, Milan (1999); and Kunsthaus Zürich (1992).

Permanent, long-term, and commissioned sculpture installations include *Large Red Sphere*, Türkentor, Kunstareal Munich, Germany (2010); *Time/Timeless/ No Time*, Chichu Art Museum, Naoshima, Japan (2004); *One Sun/34 Moons*, Nelson-Atkins Museum of Art, Kansas City, Missouri (2002); *Seen/Unseen Known/ Unknown*, Naoshima Contemporary Art Museum, Japan (2000); *5–7–9 Series*, Gemäldegalerie Berlin, Germany (1998); *French Bicentennial Sculpture (1789–1989)*, Assemblée Nationale, Paris (1990); *5 Continent Sculpture*, Daimler Art Collection, Stuttgart-Möhringen, Germany (1989); *The Broken Kilometer*, Dia Art Foundation, New York (1979); *The Vertical Earth Kilometer*, Friedrichsplatz Park, Kassel, Germany (1977); *The New York Earth Room*, Dia Art Foundation, New York (1977); and *The Lightning Field*, Dia Art Foundation, New Mexico (1977).

Exhibition and Publication History
Compiled by Chelsea Pierce

***Large Rod Series: Pedestal Rods 5, 7, 9, 11, 13** (1984)*   pages 50–51

EXHIBITED

Walter De Maria
Museum Boijmans-van Beuningen,
Rotterdam, The Netherlands
December 16, 1984–January 27, 1985

Walter De Maria
Gagosian Gallery, Madison Avenue,
New York
November 8, 2014–January 7, 2015

PUBLISHED

Beeren, Wim, ed. *Walter De Maria*.
Exh. cat. Rotterdam: Museum Boijmans-
van Beuningen, 1984.

Xavier Fourcade Gallery. *Walter De Maria:
The Large Rod Series, Circles/Rectangles
1984–1986*. Exh. cat. New York: Xavier
Fourcade Gallery, 1986.

***Large Rod Series: Square 5, 7, 9, 11, 13** (1984)*   page 53

EXHIBITED

*An American Renaissance: Painting and
Sculpture Since 1940*
Museum of Art Fort Lauderdale, Florida
January 12–March 30, 1986

*Large Rod Series: Circles/Rectangles
1984–1986*
Xavier Fourcade Gallery, New York
October 24–November 22, 1986

*Walter De Maria: Two Very Large
Presentations*
Moderna Museet, Stockholm
March 11–May 7, 1989

*Hyllningar—Moderna Museets Vänner 50
år (Tribute—Moderna Museet 50 years)*
Moderna Museet, Stockholm
May 23–August 31, 2003

*Objekt och kroppar i vila och rörelse
(Objects and bodies at rest and in motion)*
Moderna Museet, Stockholm
September 26, 2015–February 7, 2016

*Objekt och kroppar i vila och rörelse
(Objects and bodies at rest and in motion)*
Moderna Museet, Malmö
March 12–June 12, 2016

PUBLISHED

Hunter, Sam, ed. *An American
Renaissance: Painting and Sculpture Since
1940*. Exh. cat. Fort Lauderdale, FL:
Museum of Art Fort Lauderdale, 1986.

Xavier Fourcade Gallery. *Walter De Maria:
The Large Rod Series, Circles/Rectangles
1984–1986*. Exh. cat. New York: Xavier
Fourcade Gallery, 1986.

Nittve, Lars, ed. *Walter De Maria: Two Very
Large Presentations*. Exh. cat. Stockholm:
Moderna Museet, 1989.

Gagosian Gallery. *Walter De Maria:
The 5–7–9 Series*. Exh. cat. New York:
Gagosian Gallery, 1992.

Akimoto, Yuji. *Walter De Maria: Seen/
Unseen Known/Unknown*. Exh. cat.
Naoshima, Japan: Naoshima
Contemporary Art Museum, 2002.

af Petersens, Magnus. *Objekt och kroppar
i vila och rörelse (Objects and bodies at
rest and in motion)*. Exh. cat. Stockholm:
Moderna Museet, 2016.

Large Rod Series: Circle/Rectangle 5, 7, 9, 11, 13 (1986), Edition 1/2   pages 36–49

EXHIBITED

Walter De Maria: Counterpoint
Dallas Museum of Art
October 19, 2016–January 22, 2017

Walter De Maria: Surface Waves
San Francisco Museum of Modern Art
March 25–November 5, 2017

PUBLISHED

Delahunty, Gavin, ed. *Counterpoint: Sculpture, Music, and Walter De Maria's Large Rod Series.* Exh. cat. Dallas: Dallas Museum of Art, 2017.

Large Rod Series: Circle/Rectangle 5, 7, 9, 11, 13 (1985), Edition 2/2   page 55

EXHIBITED

Large Rod Series: Circles/Rectangles 1984–1986
Xavier Fourcade Gallery, New York
October 24–November 22, 1986

New Works: Walter De Maria
Arthur M. Sackler Museum, Harvard University, Cambridge, Massachusetts
January 24–March 16, 1986

L'époque, la mode, la morale, la passion: Aspects de l'art d'aujourd'hui, 1977–1987
Centre Georges Pompidou, Paris
May 21–August 17, 1987

Opere della Collezione (Works from the Collection)
Museo Cantonale d'Arte, Lugano
July 18–September 17, 2006

PUBLISHED

Xavier Fourcade Gallery. *Walter De Maria: The Large Rod Series, Circles/Rectangles 1984–1986.* Exh. cat. New York: Xavier Fourcade Gallery, 1986.

Blistène, Bernard, Catherine David, and Alfred Pacquement, eds. *L'époque, la mode, la morale, la passion: Aspects de l'art d'aujourd'hui, 1977–1987.* Exh. cat. Paris: Centre Georges Pompidou, 1987.

Szeemann, Harald, ed. *Walter De Maria: The 2000 Sculpture.* Exh. cat. Zurich: Kunsthaus Zurich, 1992.

Szeemann, Harald, ed. *Walter De Maria: The 2000 Sculpture.* Exh. cat. Berlin: Hamburger Bahnhof Museum für Gegenwart, 2000.

***Large Rod Series: Circle/Rectangle 5* (1986)**   pages 56–57

EXHIBITED

*Large Rod Series: Circles/Rectangles
1984–1986*
Xavier Fourcade Gallery/De Maria Studio
(additional installation of *Large Rod Series*
sculptures for private viewing), New York*
October 24–November 22, 1986

Walter De Maria
DASMAXIMUM KunstGegenwart,
Traunreut, Germany
Opened September 24, 2016

PUBLISHED

Xavier Fourcade Gallery. *Walter De Maria:
The Large Rod Series, Circles/Rectangles
1984–1986*. Exh. cat. New York: Xavier
Fourcade Gallery, 1986.

***Large Rod Series: Circle/Rectangle 7* (1986)**   pages 58–59

EXHIBITED

*Large Rod Series: Circles/Rectangles
1984–1986*
Xavier Fourcade Gallery/De Maria Studio
(additional installation of *Large Rod Series*
sculptures for private viewing), New York
October 24–November 22, 1986

Regard sur la Collection Asher B. Edelman
Musée Cantonal des Beaux-Arts
de Lausanne
January 12–February 11, 1990

Repeat Performance
Anthony Grant, Inc., New York
June 29–September 17, 2005

PUBLISHED

Xavier Fourcade Gallery. *Walter De Maria:
The Large Rod Series, Circles/Rectangles
1984–1986*. Exh. cat. New York: Xavier
Fourcade Gallery, 1986.

Musée Cantonal des Beaux-Arts
de Lausanne. *Regard sur la Collection
Asher B. Edelman*. Exh. cat. Lausanne:
Musée Cantonal des Beaux-Arts de
Lausanne, 1990.

California College of the Arts. *Selections
from the Frances and John Bowes
Collection*. San Francisco: Hooper & Irwin,
2008.

* *Square 5, 7, 9, 11, 13*; *Circle/Rectangle 5, 7, 9, 11, 13* (Edition 2/2); and *Circle/Rectangle 13* were installed for the exhibition *Large Rod Series: Circles/Rectangles 1984–1986* at Xavier Fourcade Gallery. Concurrently, the gallery arranged for private viewing of the following works at the De Maria Studio: *Circle/Rectangle 5*; *Circle/Rectangle 7*; *Circle/Rectangle 9*; and *Circle/Rectangle 11*. All works were later reproduced for the catalogue.

Large Rod Series: Circle/Rectangle 9 (1986)   page 61

EXHIBITED

*Large Rod Series: Circles/Rectangles
1984–1986*
Xavier Fourcade Gallery/De Maria Studio
(additional installation of *Large Rod Series*
sculptures for private viewing), New York
October 24–November 22, 1986

PUBLISHED

Xavier Fourcade Gallery. *Walter De Maria:
The Large Rod Series, Circles/Rectangles
1984–1986*. Exh. cat. New York: Xavier
Fourcade Gallery, 1986.

Large Rod Series: Circle/Rectangle 11 (1986)   pages 62–63

EXHIBITED

*Large Rod Series: Circles/Rectangles
1984–1986*
Xavier Fourcade Gallery/De Maria Studio
(additional installation of *Large Rod Series*
sculptures for private viewing), New York
October 24–November 22, 1986

Walter De Maria: 5 Kontinente Skulptur
Staatsgalerie Stuttgart
December 5, 1987–March 6, 1988

Walter De Maria: The 5–7–9 Series
Gagosian Gallery, Rome
March 22–May 29, 2012

PUBLISHED

Xavier Fourcade Gallery. *Walter De Maria:
The Large Rod Series, Circles/Rectangles
1984–1986*. Exh. cat. New York: Xavier
Fourcade Gallery, 1986.

Staatsgalerie Stuttgart. *Walter De Maria:
5 Kontinente Skulptur*. Exh. cat. Stuttgart:
Staatsgalerie Stuttgart, 1987.

Gagosian Gallery. *Walter De Maria:
Sculptures*. Rome: Gagosian Gallery, 2012.

EXHIBITED

*Large Rod Series: Circles/Rectangles
1984–1986*
Xavier Fourcade Gallery, New York
October 24–November 22, 1986

Walter De Maria
Magasin III Stockholm Konsthall, Sweden
September 11–December 11, 1988

*After Construction—Works from the
Collection*
Magasin III Stockholm Konsthall
February 24–May 5, 1994

*Magasin III Stockholm Konsthall på Arken:
Udvalgte værker frasamlingen (Selections
from the Collection)*
Arken Museum for Moderne Kunst, Ishøj,
Denmark
November 30, 1997–February 8, 1998

Extension
Magasin III Stockholm Konsthall
September 14, 2002–March 23, 2003

wizz eyelashes
Magasin III Stockholm Konsthall
September 18, 2014–June 7, 2015

PUBLISHED

Xavier Fourcade Gallery. *Walter De Maria:
The Large Rod Series, Circles/Rectangles
1984–1986*. Exh. cat. New York: Xavier
Fourcade Gallery, 1986.

Magasin III Stockholm Konsthall. *Walter
De Maria*. Exh. cat. Stockholm: Magasin III
Stockholm Konsthall, 1988.

Magasin III Stockholm Konsthall and
Arken Museum for Moderne Kunst.
*Magasin 3 Stockholm Konsthall på Arken:
Udvalgte værker frasamlingen (Selections
from the Collection)*. Exh. cat. Ishøj,
Denmark: Arken Museum for Moderne
Kunst, 1997.

EXHIBITED

Major Sculpture
Gagosian Gallery, New York
February 17–March 17, 1990

The Kiasma Collection
Museum of Contemporary Art Kiasma,
Helsinki
June 18–October 17, 1999

*Full House—The Kouri Collection and
American Minimalist Adventures*
Kiasma Museum of Contemporary Art,
Helsinki
October 17, 2008–January 18, 2009

PUBLISHED

Kiasma Museum of Contemporary Art. *Full
House: The Kouri Collection and American
Minimalist Adventures*. Exh. cat. Helsinki:
Kiasma, 2008.

Aarnio, Eija, ed. *The Kouri Collection in the
Museum of Contemporary Art Kiasma*.
Helsinki: Kiasma, 2008.

Copyright and Photography Credits

All works by Walter De Maria © 2016 Estate of Walter De Maria

All photography, unless otherwise noted below, is © 2016 Dallas Museum of Art.

Fig. 1: © Estate of Walter De Maria
Fig. 2: © Estate of Walter De Maria; photograph by Robert McKeever
Fig. 3: © Estate of Walter De Maria
Fig. 4: © Estate of Walter De Maria; photograph by Robert McKeever
Fig. 5: © Estate of Walter De Maria; photograph by John Cliett
Fig. 6: © Estate of Walter De Maria; photograph by Eric Pollitzer
Fig. 7: © Estate of Walter De Maria; photograph by Heilmann
Fig. 8: © Estate of Walter De Maria; photograph by John Cliett
Fig. 9: © Estate of Walter De Maria
Fig. 10: © Estate of Walter De Maria
Fig. 11: © Estate of Walter De Maria; photograph by Timm Rautert
Fig. 12: © The Museum of Modern Art/Licensed by SCALA / Art Resource, NY
Fig. 13: © Estate of Walter De Maria; photograph by Christian Gahl
Fig. 14: © Estate of Walter De Maria; photograph by John Cliett
Fig. 15: © Estate of Walter De Maria; photograph by Jon Abbott
Fig. 16: © Estate of Walter De Maria; photograph by Robert McKeever
Fig. 17: © Estate of Walter De Maria; photograph by Bevan Davies
Fig. 18: © 2016 C. Herscovici / Artists Rights Society (ARS), New York; photograph by Adam Baker
Fig. 19: © Estate of Walter De Maria; photograph by Haydar Koyupinar
Fig. 20: © Estate of Walter De Maria; photograph by Tomio Ohashi
Figs. 30–31: © Estate of Walter De Maria; photographs by Robert McKeever
Figs. 32–33: © Estate of Walter De Maria
Fig. 34: © Estate of Walter De Maria; photograph by Pino Musi
Figs. 35–36: © The Estate of Walter De Maria; photographs by Franz Kimmel
Figs. 37–38: © Dallas Museum of Art; photographs by Paul Kirchner
Fig. 39: © Estate of Walter De Maria; photograph by David Lubarsky
Fig. 40: © Estate of Walter De Maria; photograph by Matteo Piazza
Fig. 41: © Estate of Walter De Maria; photograph by Rob McKeever
Fig. 42: © Estate of Walter De Maria; photograph by Lennart Durehed
Fig. 43: © Estate of Walter De Maria; Finnish National Gallery

We greatly respect the protected status of all copyrighted material. We have endeavored, with due diligence, to identify and contact each copyright owner. In some cases we have been unable to trace current copyright holders. We welcome notification and will correct errors in subsequent editions.

Front and back cover: *Large Rod Series: Circle/Rectangle 5, 7, 9, 11, 13*, 1986. Edition 1/2. Stainless steel. Short rectangle configuration with 9 rods. Collection of the Dallas Museum of Art through the TWO x TWO for AIDS and Art Fund and the San Francisco Museum of Modern Art through the Phyllis C. Wattis Fund for Major Acquisitions

Published in conjunction with the installation of Walter De Maria's *Large Rod Series: Circle/Rectangle 5, 7, 9, 11, 13*, on view at the Dallas Museum of Art from October 19, 2016 to January 22, 2017, and at the San Francisco Museum of Modern Art from March 25 to November 5, 2017.

The publication has been generously underwritten by TWO x TWO for AIDS and Art, an annual fundraising event that jointly benefits amfAR, The Foundation for AIDS Research and the Dallas Museum of Art. Additional support has been provided by the Gagosian Gallery.

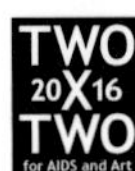 **G A G O S I A N**

Published by the Dallas Museum of Art
www.DMA.org

Distributed by Yale University Press,
New Haven and London
www.yalebooks.com/art

Produced by Miko McGinty, Inc.
www.mikomcginty.com

Dallas Museum of Art

Augustín Arteaga
The Eugene McDermott Director

Gavin Delahunty
The Hoffman Family Senior Curator of
Contemporary Art

Tamara Wootton Forsyth
Associate Director of Collections, Exhibitions,
and Facilities Management

Eric Zeidler
Publications Manager

Chelsea Pierce
Curatorial Administrative Assistant

Edited by Ellen Hirzy
Designed by Miko McGinty
Typeset in Fakt by Tina Henderson
Printed and bound in Italy by Trifolio SRL

Library of Congress
Cataloging-in-Publication Data

Names: Dallas Museum of Art, author. | Delahunty, Gavin, editor. | De Maria, Walter, 1935–2013. | San Francisco Museum of Modern Art.
Title: Counterpoint : sculpture, music, and Walter De Maria's Large rod series / edited by Gavin Delahunty ; with essays by Gavin Delahunty, Caitlin Haskell ; with contributions by Chelsea Pierce, Jason Treuting ; and with installation notes by Walter De Maria.
Description: Dallas : Dallas Museum of Art, 2017. | "Published in conjunction with the installation of Walter De Maria's Large Rod Series: Circle/Rectangle 5, 7, 9, 11, 13, on view at the Dallas Museum of Art from October 19, 2016 to January 22, 2017, and at the San Francisco Museum of Modern Art from March 25 to November 5, 2017." | Includes bibliographical references.
Identifiers: LCCN 2016041240 | ISBN 9780300225730 (hardcover : alk. paper)
Subjects: LCSH: De Maria, Walter, 1935–2013. Large rod series—Catalogs. | De Maria, Walter, 1935–2013. Pure polygon series—Catalogs.
Classification: LCC NB237.D47 A67 2017 | DDC 709.2—dc23
LC record available at https://lccn.loc.gov/2016041240